Total Exposure

PIECES OF ME

PAMELA LONG

Total Exposure/Pieces of Me

For information contact: rochelleadams07@gmail.com

Typesetting by Sally Hanan of Inksnatcher.com
Cover by Elizabeth Moore/IG page @wlmliz
Head shot by Michael Isiah King

Total Exposure: Pieces of Me/Pamela Long
ISBN: 978-0-578-687552-0
eBook ISBN: 978-0578-70009-0

This book is dedicated to the heartbeat of my life,
Jesus Christ, the Son of God.

Contents

Disclaimer

This book entails real events that has occurred in my life. In no way, shape or form have I opened up the secrets of my heart to degrade or diminish the reputation of others. This book was written solely on the premise of me becoming free and freeing others.

This is the truth and nothing but the truth, so help me God.

Grace carried me here and by grace I'll carry on.

—Unknown

Note from Pamela

This book contains small flashbacks of my life that may help to inspire someone to find the strength to stand up and break free from their past. Sometimes all a person needs to get started is a spark, not the entire fire. May this short book cause a spark within you that will lead to your freedom. We can obtain freedom together one step and one tear at a time. The first step to obtaining freedom is not going out and telling the whole world your story, but it's acknowledging that it happened and then telling yourself that you won't allow it to have rule and dominion over you any longer.

Looking into the mirror of your life can really be discouraging at first because the mirror exposes everything, but there is an upside to standing in the mirror naked and unclothed. If you look into the mirror with the intent of seeing yourself as one who has a purpose, you'll see that every flaw and imperfection has contributed to making you the great person that you are today. I know that it may not be the picture of perfection that you want right now, but if you would be honest about the person you see in the mirror, it can be your transitional moment into the person God intended for you to become. Are you willing to journey with me to an unfamiliar place that may hold the key to your destiny? If so, let's do it! You're not alone.

We're in this together.

Pamela

Prologue

What are people going to say if I tell everything? Will I be ridiculed for my truth? Will I be hated because of my transparency that may cause those that hurt me to be angered? All these grueling thoughts traipse back and forth through my mind as I write, but I swallow and continue. I am so old school. *Chuckling to myself.* What I mean by that is, I have this expensive laptop that I've purchased, and I quickly bypass it and pick up a pen and pad and get to writing. *Hold up a minute.* This pen is saying more than what I intended because there are some things I wasn't planning on sharing, but my heart won't shut up. It is telling my pen all of the pain and dirt that I went through. As I go back and read over what's been written I tell myself, *Maybe I've said too much,* but in my heart of hearts I know I must release every word regardless of the outcome. The truth is the truth.

Throughout this adventure called life, I've realized that the word "truth" has a way of causing mayhem to those who walk in deception. This five-letter word has the power to make a person go off the deep end especially when there are hidden pieces involved. At this pivotal point of my life I've come to the conclusion that I will speak my truth without anyone's permission. It's time for me to live and sail the way that I was created, but before I sail, I must first shed the layers of life that stole my luster. As my father once told me, "If me telling the truth puts a yoke around someone's neck that's between them and God, not me." In all honesty there were a few times that I thought about coloring up some of the story and painting a pretty picture so that it wouldn't be so ugly, but if I did that I'd still be bound. It would be a smoking mirror; the appearance of truth but its equity would be a whole lie. No more hidden secrets, No more masquerading, and definitely No more fake smiles. I've sat back long enough and watched so many people live double lives without saying one word, but there comes a time when it's time to speak and that time is now. I've made a conscience decision to tell my story and by me doing so may cause eyes to roll, tempers to flare, and even hurtful words to be said about me personally, but I have come to this resolve. I no longer live for people's approval. Outside opinions will no longer govern my life. They may hurt at times and I may even shed a tear because of them but moving forward is a must. It's too many lives on the line to care about the few who'll be mad because they no longer can control me.

Please understand that when you decide to be bold and stand and speak up for yourself, you may come face-to-face with wanting to cower. But you have to remind yourself that you're not doing anything wrong. While writing I could sometimes hear and feel that frightened little girl saying, "Maybe you should hold your mule," *which means that I should just keep my mouth shut.* But if I do, the devil wins and people remain trapped that may have gotten free if I stood my ground and spoke up. I can no longer be quiet. I've been chosen to sound the alarm and let others know that we no longer have to be silent. Freedom can be obtained if we are willing to go through the process. It is time to reclaim all that was stolen, but before we can get back what's been stolen, we must first admit what has been done to us. And then we must also be ready to admit the part we've allowed, *which I believe is the hardest,* because it makes us aware of our faults in the situation, if any. There was a time when I told myself that I would carry all my secrets to the grave, but God had a different plan. What I desired to forget about and let sleeping dogs lie, God said someone needs your story so that they too can live! This is why I can't and won't be driven by my feelings.

Freedom is our portion.

1

Ugly Girl

WHO WANTS TO PLAY hide and go get it? This was a game we had no business playing, but we did. It involved a boy chasing down a girl of his desire and once she was caught, he was rewarded by humping her a few times and then she'd run off and the chase would start all over again. Because of us knowing what we were doing was wrong, we had to be cautious and plan carefully, so the humping took place in the woods. If any adult would have seen what we were doing, can someone say, "Early grave!" That's exactly what all of us would have experienced, six feet under! We would have gotten our butts beaten *especially me* and for a very long time. That beating would have come by the hand of my babysitter, my grandmother, who stayed in her window watching us like a hawk. She had what I call "laser sharp vision." This woman could see through walls, well at least that's what I thought. But on the particular days I made the decision to play this game, she was blinded from our escapades. I don't know what possessed me to play with fire knowing that my grandmother was the "I see everything queen." I can't believe I made a conscious decision to play Russian roulette knowing that my Grammy was a no-nonsense kind of woman. She had belts, switches, and broomsticks at her fingertips. She was known in the community as the one person you didn't play with, and my silly behind decided to play a humping game right up under her nose. *Really, Pam*? This is one of the reasons why I know there is a God in heaven, and he watches over dummies. Had she caught wind of what was going on, I would have had a short life. You know something? I never took the time to tell God thank you for hiding me from my grandmother on that day. *Thank you, Lord.* I believe that God knew if my grandmother saw me partaking in such activities, she would have halfway killed me. So, I think even though I was completely wrong, God hid me from her wrath, which would have put a bad hurting on my two little buns.

Now as the boys gave chase, the girls would scream and holler as they got close to catching us, but there was something that I quickly noticed. There were very few boys chasing me, if any.

"Here I am!"

"Chase me!"

"You can't catch me!"

"I'm over here!"

Back then, because of how I thought about myself, I'm sure these words swarmed my mind as I watched the boys chase down all the other girls on the basketball court and throughout the playground. I wasn't one of the ones who was frequently caught, but I wanted to be. I wasn't even one of the fourth or fifth who were chased. I was more like the last. I wasn't really popular when it came to looks. I was deemed as the skinny dark girl who didn't have a butt, *and those words cut like a knife.* I always felt like the ugly duckling. The black swan of the group. There is not a time that I can recall feeling pretty. It seemed like the only boys who chased me were the ones all the girls thought were unattractive, and I did not want one of them catching me. That was definitely a no-no. Me being caught by one of the unpopular boys would be terrible. I wanted the boy who all the little girls were head over heels for to catch me, not the boy no one liked.

I honestly knew that playing this game wasn't right, but I wanted to be a part of what was going on. I wasn't a leader at all. I was quite the follower. All of my friends were playing, so I made the decision to do the same. I actually was ready and willing to be caught, but only by the boys I desired.

As a kid I didn't see that playing this game was something that was bad. But what I did know was that if an adult saw us, we were going down. So just like everything else I did that was wrong, I hid it (*no* one would *ever find out* and that was cool with me.) One thing I didn't know was that this behavior I played out in my childhood would have so many damaging effects on my future. If only I knew what I know now, I promise you, I would have gone in another direction.

Back to the chase—what I did after dodging one of the unpopular boys is very interesting to me. I made it my business not be caught by one of them, but when one of the cute boys was in close proximity, I would openly run or hide behind a tree, with hopes of being caught. But most of the time they ran right past me to chase the pretty girl or the one who was thicker than me. *Why is he still trying to catch her and I'm right here?* I wanted to be caught by him. *What's wrong with me?*

Being caught by one of the popular boys, would have at least been an indicator that I was pretty too. Even with my feelings being hurt because of being overlooked, I would continue to play with the hopes of being caught by one of the boys I was crushing on. Oh shoot, the cute guy has finally caught me, but it's only because all the other girls are running too fast. Even though I'm not his first pick, and I know he wanted to catch someone else, it's okay, I'll take it.

Question

What happens to a young girl who grows up with misconceptions about herself? She grows up to be a woman with the same misconceptions. The only thing that has evolved is her age. She still has the same unhealthy thoughts that cloud her mind as she continues to wait to be chased by the cute boys. I remember being in my teenage years. I wanted to alter my entire appearance because of feeling so beat down by my own thoughts and other people's perceptions of me, that I desired to be someone else. It seemed like all I ever heard was how black, skinny, and ugly I was. The only person that ever told me I was pretty was my mama and that gets old and played out. Especially when you're waiting on the boy you were crushing on to at least acknowledge you. There were times that I wanted lighter skin because I thought dark skin was ugly. Someone of the same race was always saying, "You are so dark!" I desired to have what some call 'good hair' because I thought my hair was thick and nappy. I also wanted slimmer and chinky eyes, a thick body, and I even wanted smaller feet because this is what I thought the boys wanted. "Maybe if I changed my appearance, I would become desirable to the boys." These were the grueling thoughts that pierced my mind. Everything that I saw the boys chasing after was everything I was not, so I made it my focus to become what the boys chased. "If only I had lighter skin, thinner hair, and a round butt they'd all want me". This is one of many lies that I had convinced myself of, and these thoughts became my focus both day and night. I wanted to be transformed into a new girl, but every morning I woke up and saw the same dark-skinned girl looking back at me as I stood in the mirror. "Why would God make me this way? Why do I have to be the ugly one?"

I was so distraught over my looks that I began to think unrealistically about being different. "What if I was a boy?" If I was a boy I wouldn't have to worry about this quest for beauty. All I would have to worry about is dressing really fly and making sure that I brushed my hair to make the waves spin. So, when I had time to myself, I would practice being a boy. I would stand in the mirror with my hair tucked into a baseball cap. With baggy jeans on and a hoodie, I would then place a pair of socks in my pants so that I could have the bulge that made it seem like I had a penis. After I got my look together, I would take my stance in the mirror and start to speak in a low-registered voice, grab on my pants in the crotch area, and begin to emulate what I saw my brother do. *Wait a minute!" I'm tripping!* Even though I knew that I was tripping, I was still hurting. All I wanted was to be considered and accepted as one of the pretty girls and I would have been good. *Why don't they notice me?* Dang! I would have even opted for someone to just say that I was cute. That's how bad I wanted to feel wanted. I was starving to just be considered. My way of thinking had become completely unstable. My silent thoughts not only caused me pain, but they were poisoning my view.

We all know that if a person is not helped immediately when poisoned, death could be their fate. No one knew or understood that there was a part of me dying every day. The thing dying was my love for myself. I felt like if I couldn't be the light-skinned big booty girl that all the boys wanted, then I guess becoming a boy was meant to be.

I remember one time I went outside dressed like a boy. It was nighttime and I was dressed in all black walking with one of my guy friends. A car pulled up and asked for directions or something like that. He said, "Excuse me fella, can you give me directions?" I don't remember the exact location he was looking for, but when I answered him back, I made sure he heard these words, "I am not a boy!" I was so offended. It didn't feel good to be called something I wasn't. Needless to say, I got over that hump quickly, but my chase for beauty was still haunting me as I set out daily to obtain it.

Saddened and living in my own small reality, I had come to the conclusion that I was ugly and that I was going to stay ugly for the rest of my life. I was such a happy and miserable girl. Such an oxymoron, right? I was one of the jolliest little girls around! I was vibrant and full of life, but as I grew and became aware of people's opinion of me, I began to dislike who I was.

I no longer had to hear someone say the word "ugly" to me because I was fully convinced that I was. The word was stamped and sealed in my mind like a stamp on a postcard. It was so embedded in my thoughts that every time I stood in front of a mirror and thought I was cute, it would point out every flaw, and that quickly made me feel defeated. There were days when I thought I had it going on and then I would get a dose of reality: I'd see the light-skinned girl walk past the boys in the hallway at school, and their response was that of an uproar. Their reaction toward her told me that I was ugly because when I walked by, they didn't respond to me like that. "What's up, P?" *Really? Is that all I get? Whatever!!!* To say the least, I was very angry and upset about their reaction towards me. I was jealous and upset about what had taken place, but I didn't say anything. And on top of all that, I also realized that my body was different from all the other girls'. They were all soft and fluffy, built with full faces and full bodies, and here I was with muscles and strength like He-Man. Why? I saw no similarities in any of my friends, and because of that I just knew I was ugly. I constantly stood in the mirror wanting to be someone else. The girl looking back at me was so rejected, hurt, and lost. I felt like if there was any way I could feel beautiful, I was willing to take that route, no matter the cost. If it called for me altering myself and tailor-making a new me, I was all in.

Being rejected by the boys was a hard slap in the face, but there were some closer to me who helped seal the deal with how I saw myself. There were people in my own family who called me ugly. It's one thing to hear you're ugly from an outsider, but to hear it from within your camp is even worse. The word ugly has been a resounding song in my ears for years.

Why am I different? Why, Why, Why, Why, Why? There seemed to be no answer. The more I thought about it, the sadder I became. I was the sore thumb that always stood out. It seemed as if there was never a place for the ugly girl. The only time there was a place for me is when I was being mishandled or abused. (You'll hear about that later on.) The more I pressed to fit in, the more I stuck out. All I wanted was to feel pretty. Was I wrong for wanting to hear what I didn't know? I truly believe that I am neither the first nor the last to feel this way. I am a voice—a voice for myself and for others who may be afraid to say it themselves.

This type of hurt can take someone to a place of no return. Let me explain what I mean. There are some whom we, the world, have witnessed become totally different people right before our eyes. And I believe it is from a lack of self-love. Somewhere along the line, these particular people probably felt ugly, unloved, or not good enough and have found comfort in altering what they saw in the mirror. They believed it to be the cure for rejection, not realizing that the pain was beyond skin deep. This is why in some cases the altering continues. Alterations don't heal wounds. It's just a different mask that covers the little girl or little boy that is still hurting on the inside. Please don't think for a moment that I am putting anyone on blast concerning his or her decisions, because if I'd had the money at that time in my life, I would have done the same thing.

Right now, I'm trying to help someone understand that it's your soul that needs to be healed, not your face or body. *You are beautiful* just the way you are. Let me ask you a question. Why is it so easy for you to believe a lie quicker than the truth? Just because someone called you ugly, why would you believe that? But when you hear someone say that you're beautiful, you dismiss it and kept agreeing with false information about yourself. It's time to stop allowing outside opinions to shape your thinking. We all have been created the way God intended.

I have never heard God say that any person he made was ugly. I may not be everybody's flavor of the month but I'm fearfully and wonderfully made. Beauty is in the eye of the beholder. And one man's beauty may not be another man's viewpoint, but it does not diminish the value of the one beholding what he sees. Beauty is supposed to be embraced not compared. To be honest, real beauty is not seen but rather experienced. Outer beauty fades but hidden beauty always shines through, because there is nothing that can dim its light.

I'm not saying that we don't have to take care of ourselves, but I am saying, don't allow someone to tell you what you are and what you're not. With all of that being said, head up, shoulders back, and now walk with a high step that I call sah'shay! It's time to shed the old and encounter our new.

It's interesting how such a small word can cause so much damage. It also has the power to chase a person for a lifetime, when not confronted. Please understand that negative words have an agenda. Speaking negatively tears down and breaks down anyone or anything in its path. I was a victim who was tortured mentally for years by this four-letter word that I embraced. It was so deep in the mental recesses of my mind that when I heard someone refer to me as pretty, there was no room for belief in what they were trying to convey. I was already convinced that it was a lie.

When I stood in the mirror it was there. When I met a cute guy, it was there. And even when I got married it continued to show me no slack. This small word had formed such a huge stronghold in my mind that it was all I saw and heard even when others weren't talking. It showed up at the most inopportune times and it showed me no mercy. From childhood to adolescence, and now into adulthood the struggle has been real. People say that words don't hurt. They actually go beyond hurt. They crush, demolish, and replay over and over again in your head. These words have the ability to take one's physical life if not dealt with. Remember that old saying, "Sticks and stones may break my bones, but names will never hurt me?" I think I would have rather gotten hit with the sticks and stones because at least it would have healed a few days later. I've carried this hurt from childhood. Words have the potential to not only wound, but to destroy when they have a negative connotation. A friend of mine told me that words don't have a sense of humor. So, with that being said, I suggest you watch your words.

By God's grace, I am learning how to love and appreciate myself daily. I now love my athletic build, my dark skin, my smile, and all the other things about me that were once hard for me to look at. I have discovered that before I can see beauty, I must first know that I am beautiful. And today I know it more than I've ever known.

Below is my new definition of the word ugly:

U

Gotta

Love

Yourself

PS You're Beautiful.

2

The Predator

I WAS A LOVING KID who was friendly and kind to everyone I met, but sometimes my friendliness was a problem for my mom. The reason why my friendliness became a problem for her was because I pretty much would hug and kiss everyone around me.

I was this sweet kid who didn't have a mean streak in my body, that loved and kissed on everyone that came to our house. Being that I was so loving, when it was time for guests or any family member to leave our house, I would pucker up and kiss them goodbye. My mom would be outraged! She'd tell them sternly, "Do not kiss my baby on her lips!" Afterwards she would take me into the bathroom where she'd wash my lips off with soap and admonish me to stop kissing people. I didn't know that it was wrong to kiss them. I was just following my little heart. With my feelings being hurt I would tell her, "Okay," and then go about my business. But a few days later I would be puckering up again. This time, because I disobeyed. I got in trouble for not listening, but it didn't make me completely stop kissing people. I don't know why I was the kid who expressed herself in this way, but I did.

There was one person I didn't like kissing and that was one of my older cousins who was old enough to be my grandfather. He sometimes had a little too much to drink, and when he was drunk, he would become emotional and begin to express how he loved his family (which he did). After expressing his love, he would start to kiss all of us. This wasn't a good look, but you guessed right. I kissed him anyway.

There's now someone new on the scene, who has become a frequent visitor in our house. He doesn't receive kisses from me, but he does gain my trust. His presence in our home had become a regular routine. He was there so much that he no longer really needed to knock on the door in order to enter, but he still did. Everybody liked him. I liked him a lot because he was nice, and he always brought things for us. He would take us out to the movies, skating, White Castles, Burger King, McDonald's and so many other places that was a kid's dream. He seemed harmless. There was nothing about him that gave my mama or my Grandma, who had x-ray vision, a bad feeling. The more he came around, the more comfortable I became with him. He had become a permanent fixture in the house, so being around him was now normal. Maybe it was because he was like a daddy figure to me. I remember the times I sat on his lap to play, fell asleep, or sat and watched TV.

Nothing ever seemed to be out of line, but somewhere along the line, something happened to you, and you became very different with me.

I was this kid with a tremendous heart who took to you quickly. Wow! I say wow because as I continued to grow up, I still had this tremendously caring heart that I entrusted to all the wrong people. And I found myself suffering the consequences of my actions. Why was something always happening to me? That's the question I'm sure many of us would like to have an answer to. Was there a sign over my head that said, "Destroy this kid, or was it something deeper?" I guess we'll soon find out.

Then one day things were different. Something changed. I can't really put my finger on what happened, but the events that follow will describe exactly what I mean. I had no clue that something different was going on. I was just being a kid. I had no idea that he was a wolf in sheep's clothing.

To every mother: Little girls should not be able to play on the lap of a man. What may seem to be very innocent for the child can be an arousal for them. I'm not saying this is the case concerning every man because it's not, but there are some wackos out here who are perverted and in need of deliverance from sexual demons. You have to take precaution!

Be on guard, stay watchful, and protect your babies. I also urge you to watch your little boys as well because some predators don't have a sexual preference. My mother was by far one of the greatest mothers that ever lived, but my predator got past her. Don't trust anyone when it comes to your babies! Scrutinize everyone and make no apologies for it. You have been called to protect!

At the age of eight or nine, *I don't recall the exact age, things became a little more intense.* He graduated from sitting me on his lap to touching me. I honestly don't remember where he touched me or what he did, but I did know is that it was inappropriate. I was scared, but him with his manipulating ways told me that this was "our little secret." He was very smart about how he did things because touching me wasn't something he did every time he saw me. I believe he got nervous because he knew that I knew, something was wrong. But he made sure he stayed in my ear telling me that he was just playing with me, and because I trusted him, even though I knew something wasn't right, I went with it.

After a while he started coming to my room and touching. I hated seeing him standing there. Even though I wasn't happy about what was going on, I still didn't tell anyone what he was doing to me. And due to me not telling on him, things began to happen more frequently, which I despised. By this time he had convinced me that we were only playing a game, and it was just between us.

> My stomach is doing flips because I am holding back tears as I write. This sick punk took complete advantage of me! This caused me so much turmoil in my life.
>
> As a little girl I was afraid of the dark, and as an adult I struggled for years, when I turned my lights off. I often thought that something was waiting for me. Could all of the fear that I housed on the inside, have come from his nighttime visits? That's when he did most of his prowling.

Addressing You Personally

What made this so complicated and heart wrenching was the fact that I loved you very much, and so did everyone else. Despite your illness, how could this be? You were the one who helped everyone. Who would have ever thought, you played secret games with me? You made sure I was always okay, and this played a major part in me trusting you. You made yourself seem like a friend who was always there. So why would I tell on you and get you into trouble? In all honesty, you were a sick bastard that needed help, and no one saw through your diabolical and twisted ways. You mastered in hiding the real you. I don't know why you chose me, but in my heart, I know that there were others. You had children of your own who were just a little older than me, and I truly believe they are victims as well. What happened to you to make you become this monster? Who or what enticed you to touch on little kids? You have a son! What if you did the same thing to him that you've done to me? I am getting so angry right now, but instead of me doing what I feel, which is cussing you out, I'll do what you need most, *pray!*

I need to take a minute and pray for myself as well, because I said something about you in the heat of the moment that I shouldn't have said. I could have chosen to address you differently. So for that I ask God to forgive me. Lord God, please forgive me for calling him a bastard, because I know that cussing is wrong. But I didn't want to curb my tongue or sugar coat what I thought of him in this moment. This man stole so much from me and had no remorse for taking away my innocence. But even in all of this, he needs you, Lord. You are a God who forgives to the utmost! I have been guilty of much myself, but by the blood of Jesus, I have been forgiven and I pray the same for those who hurt me. The arms of Jesus are open to all who will come.

I had my days when I wanted to tell someone, but I was too ashamed. I thought it was my fault. You made it seem like it was normal behavior between a man and a child, so I did what you requested. The wrong thing became the right thing and after a while it stole my voice, and I become a mute who allowed any and everything to be done to me. Your plot was to get me to trust you and when you got close enough you silenced me, which gave you rulership to have your way.

I'm now around thirteen or fourteen and I'm beginning to like boys. I have a boyfriend now and we've kissed here and there but nothing too heavy. But there still lies this disgusting little problem ... YOU! Are you really still trying to come at me? *I hate this*! I have a boyfriend now. Aren't you tired of this? *I know I am. I want to tell someone what's going on so bad, but I don't.*

Here we go again with you calling me upstairs pretending you need me to get you something. What do you want? You want me to what? I don't clearly remember what you asked, but I do recall there being times that I was in the bed with you while you grinded on me. I'm not sure if you ever asked me to handle your penis with my hands, but there were those times when things escalated, when your penis was in my hand.

There are some things you did to me that are so clear in my mind. And then, there are some things that you did, that I don't even remember. But there is one thing I know for sure. The stuff you did with and to me was absolutely wrong.

I can honestly say that you touching me, and me touching you, was something I never wanted to do. But after a while, I got used to it.

Eventually, you would talk me into doing something I didn't want to do, and once I finished allowing you to do whatever you felt, I left. These visits had now become so routine that I started looking for you. I was brainwashed! It was almost like I was anticipating whatever you had in mind to do to me for the day.

When I thought that things couldn't get any worse, I remember the day you asked me to let you rub your penis across my butt. I didn't want to because that was taking it too far. You kept pleading with me and telling me you wouldn't do anything except rub it on me. The catch was that you wanted to rub it on my bare skin. That day I told you no, but you repeatedly asked me and a few days later, I gave in. You promised me you wouldn't try anything else, so I got under your covers and pulled down my pants and laid on my stomach. You began to rub your penis on my butt and then asked if you could rub it on my inner thighs from behind. I told you yes. As you laid on me you were making all of these weird sounds and kissing on my ear. I was so petrified, that I just laid there stiff as you began to put your leg in between mine to try and spread my legs apart. You continued to rub your penis across my inner thighs and before I knew it, I felt your penis by the hole of my vagina. I clinched up and you whispered you weren't going to push it in. You were just rubbing it on me, so I laid there in silence. The next thing I know you were pressing into my vagina trying to penetrate me but that's when I had enough. I closed my legs and you stopped trying to penetrate me, but you stuck your penis in between my thighs and began to pump on me until you ejaculated. After you finished, you kissed my ear, rolled off of me, and I got up and left.

After that encounter you tried to get me alone every time you saw me. I did all that I could to avoid you, but sometimes it was inevitable. This time when you got me alone you quickly had me lay down on my stomach. You tried to penetrate me right away but couldn't get it in, so I lay on my arm and made a little fist. You put your penis in my hand and that satisfied you enough to leave me alone.

There was one time when you wanted to lay on top of me, face-to-face (*tears*). I couldn't even look at you. I put my head to the side and covered my face as you lay on top of me. This time you pushed your penis inside of me. It somewhat went in and then it came back out.

Once that happened, I left. I'd had enough and I wasn't going to do this anymore and I meant it. Every once in a while, you would say something slick, but no longer did you try to touch me. Maybe it was because you saw the hate in my eyes that I had for you, and at any given moment I could have exploded. What a sick jerk you were! It's not easy writing this because it brings back so many unwanted memories. But if my truth helps someone else, then it's all worth reliving the pain.

I was emotionally and mentally jacked up for a long time. I blamed myself for everything that happened. I was afraid people would say it was all my fault, so I kept it all inside until now. You opened up a door in me that is only lawful for a husband and wife. You gave me something no young girl should ever have, and that was a sexual appetite and insecurities. My thoughts of myself were damaged. The only thing I thought I was good for was lying on my back. My self-esteem was shot, my confidence level was at a zero, and my love for myself was non-existent. I struggled for years trying to love myself and not use my vagina as a weapon toward dudes who claimed they loved me. I was a hurt young girl, who grew into a hurt teen, who turned into a hurt woman. But God loved me back to life! Not only did he heal me, he also showed me how to forgive the person who stole years upon years of my life.

I remember the day you went into the hospital. You had no one to be there for you. I believe and know it was God stripping you of everything and everyone. But guess who he used to be there? Pamela. It was only God who put it in my heart to be there for you. I cooked food, told you that Jesus loved you and visited you quite often while you were in the hospital. Who does this? A child of God whose heart has been changed by the power of God, that's who.

> Dear Predator,
>
> It took some time to be able to look you in the face and not hate you. After all the hurt you caused, there was no way I should have been able to forgive you, but I do. Forgiveness was not for you but for me. If I would have held on to the pain you caused, I would have become bitter and stagnated in my life. Even though you took advantage of me, my misery has become a message to help others.
>
> Please know that one day you will stand before God and give an account of all you've done in your life. I hope and pray that you repented for what you did to me. I remember the day I finally got up the nerve and asked you why you did what you did to me. The look on your face was blank and you didn't even respond. I told

you that I forgave you, and I loved you, and that you needed to go to God before it was too late and then I left. That day I regained some of me and today I am completely whole. I am so thankful that Jesus is able to do the impossible! That day when I stood there looking in your face, I saw the true state of your life. I saw a wretched soul in need of a loving Savior! Jesus is the answer! He specializes in saving the unsaved. I remember when you got sick and was on your death bed and the fear of dying was all over you. As I spoke to you about salvation in Jesus Christ, you said you believed. I really believe in my heart that you accepted Christ into your heart before you died, and that was and is the beauty about your life.

I really don't know how I could even stomach to look at you, from a human standpoint. But when Jesus comes into a heart, he transforms it into his likeness. All I knew was that, this man cannot die without repenting and asking Jesus to cleanse him of his sins and to save him. It was no longer about what you did to me, but your soul. I give God all the glory, honor and praise for being a God who is able to forgive every kind of sin.

And to the master craftsman who was behind all of this evil—the devil,

You lost!!!

3

The Party House

THE MUSIC IS ON BLAST, the food is on the grill, and all the kids are running amok, while most of the grown-ups are sipping on drinks. Cigarette smoke is in the air, and the living room floor has become an instant dance floor for the old and the young. The record player is spinning oldies but goodies for the grown folks, and the radio is blaring Michael Jackson, which has every kid in the house trying to moonwalk. These were the good old days when having fun was innocent. The party house was the place to be and everyone knew it. When my family got together it pulled people out of the wood works from near and far.

The house would be full of family and friends, but every once in a while, someone who lived in the community, who wasn't invited, would come moseying on in. You would immediately see heads of some of my family members turning and their eyes watching to see what was up with this person.

Once the air cleared and everyone gave the notion that they were okay to stay, the festivities continued.

I truly miss that innocence. Nowadays, fun for some of these knucklehead kids is shooting or stabbing people, videotaping fights, sex tapes, and popping mollies. Our kids are in a state of emergency! It is time for us to wake up and help these babies before it's too late. I digress for now, but I hope someone hears me.

It's finally the weekend and it's about to go down. It is time to clean up and get ready to go and have some fun. I'm prepared to have a good time as long as I don't have to spend the night. How could such a fantastic time turn into straight boredom? I thought it would have been nonstop fun staying the night at the party house, but it wasn't. We were like hostages. We couldn't do anything! When we went outside, we had to stay in the front yard, and if we were in the back of the house we could only go as far as the clothesline. *Dang*! Can we breathe and play like kids? We couldn't run, we couldn't laugh too loud, we couldn't, we couldn't, we couldn't, was all we heard! Everything was stop or no. This wasn't it at all. I was ready to go back home but when I thought about. I'd rather be outside talking to my friends by the clothesline than be stuck in the house being treated like a baby.

Just when I thought it couldn't get any worse.

Streetlights!

Once the streetlights came on, it was a wrap. My mama had this rule that whenever the streetlights came on, we had to be either inside the house or on the step.

Imagine playing around the neighborhood with your friends. The sky is bright and suddenly you see that streetlight come on. It is time to run! You better get ready to do the 100-yard dash in sixty seconds or less, because if that light turned on without me being present on the front or back step. It was grounds for a guaranteed butt whoopin'. Really? The streetlights came on about an hour before it got dark and guess where I was. In the yard while everyone else played. This must have been a family tradition because my cousins had to do the same thing.

All of my little friends would be running around free while I called them over to the clothesline to talk and play. How embarrassing! I can say this now because I'm older, but I snuck away from that clothesline a few good times. Thank God I didn't get caught because had I gotten caught. As Marvin Sapp said, I never would have made it.

Even though spending the night at the party house was whack, we made it fun, especially when some of the other kids stayed over. Reflecting back on these days makes me miss being a kid. My family knew how to party and entertain one another. We were such a tight-knit family, nothing or no one could break us apart. We may have fought among ourselves sometimes, but no outsider better not have tried it, because that's when the poop would hit the fan.

> If I could go back in time, the party house would definitely be one of the houses I'd love to visit. I would open up the door and go straight into the living room and start dancing like we used to. I'd also get the chance to see all my family members who've passed on to glory. What a moment that would be, to smile with them again for one night.

Now that the day was well spent, the grown-ups began to discuss what was next on their agenda, and that meant that the kids had to go upstairs and play. That sucked! I wanted to be in the middle of everything. Especially in the midst of the adults. I wasn't trying to be grown, I was just fascinated by what they were doing, and I wanted in. They played cards, drank liquor, smoked cigarettes, cussed, laughed, and told hilarious jokes. I wanted to sit and laugh even though I was too young to understand what I would've been laughing at. I just wanted to be a part of what I thought was fun.

Growing up in my family we had rules. I don't know about y'all, but when the grown-ups were ready for grown people fun, the kids had to go. And if you acted like you wanted to be hardheaded and stay when you were told to leave, it would cost you a five to ten. A five to ten is a whoopin' that lasted for about five to ten minutes, and it was something you would remember for a long time.

Now if you were anything like me, getting beat was something I didn't fancy at all, but I always found myself getting my butt tore up more often then I may have wanted. My aim wasn't to get in trouble, but trouble was always on the way.

Getting back into that living room was a must for me. I would creep back downstairs to get an ear full of what was being said. As I stood there silently watching, and smelling the cigarette smoke, I was amazed and in awe because though I could barely see the things that went on, I did get the chance to see the people who were standing on the floor around the card table.

This makes me think of the times when we had our family cookouts at my aunt's house. *Those were some of the greatest times.* I had so much fun, especially when I wasn't getting into trouble. I was always doing something I should not have been doing. My moment of mischievousness would quickly be interrupted by the voice of my mama piercing through asking, "What were you told to do?" As I stood there trying to conjure up thoughts and prepare myself to lie and ask all these fake questions, she beat me to the punch almost every time.

"Go somewhere and sit yourself down, before I beat your tail!"

I was out! I would fly out of her sight immediately. To say the least, I was embarrassed because all the adults were in total agreement with what my mama said. I felt so small. But even with me feeling the way I did, how many of y'all know it wasn't over yet. You already know ya girl had to push the last button.

I was so hardheaded as a kid. I wanted things done my way, and most of the time, my way caused me great pain. Even with the pain that it caused, I still insisted on doing things my way.

With that backdrop, you can understand why getting back downstairs for me was a must. Who cares that it may cost me a good old fashioned beatdown? I wanted what I wanted, and I was dead set on it.

God, please help me, if I get caught.

The Games We Played

Now, while the adults were busy having fun

downstairs, us kids had a few games of our own. One of the games we played was for kids only. No adults could play, nor could they know anything about this game because it would have led to all of us getting in a lot of trouble. The game we played was called the kissing game. The girls would lie down on the bed, and the boys would lie on top of us and we'd kiss. There were specific rules to the game. All the kissing and laying on top of each other had to take place in the dark. One person was in control of the lights and someone else was appointed to yell out the word switch. When the person yelled switch, the boy would leave the girl he was on top of and get on top of another girl and begin to kiss her. Sometimes the light controller turned the lights on a little early, I think they did that to see what people were doing.

I remember seeing that some of the older girls who had breasts had their boobies on display. They also were allowing the boys to feel them up. I saw one of the older boys on top of one girl's pants, and he had his pants down. (Whoa.) This was a bit much, but being that I was so young, I laughed quietly and stared really hard at what I was seeing.

Every kid in the room had to participate because if one kid didn't have any involvement, it left room for them to go home and tell their parents what went on. I guess this was the way the older kids kept us younger ones quiet.

Oh shoot! There is another person I forgot to mention, the lookout. The job of the lookout person was the most crucial. They were the ones who stood at the top of the stairs and alarmed those of us in the room when a grown-up was coming. Now don't think for a minute that the lookout person didn't have their share in the room because they did. Remember I told you we all had to participate.

Every once in a while, an adult would come upstairs to use the bathroom, and the lookout person would let those of us in the room know that trouble was near. In that time, all shameful activity would cease. Sometimes one of the adults who used the bathroom would open the door to see what we were up to. Did you catch that? They walked right in, no knocking. If they would have found that door locked, our butts would have been broken into pieces. The grown-up, who more than likely was a relative, would peer around the room to see our faces. Some stayed and talked for a minute, while others just looked inside then closed the door. Whew, close call.

I don't know how they didn't feel the nervousness in the room, but I thank God that they didn't. Had they known what was taking place seconds before them opening up that door, we would have been whooped, beat, and mauled. We would have gotten the blood beat out of us, literally.

#Dead

It's something how a night of innocence turned into years of secrecy. It wasn't planned and it definitely wasn't something discussed, but it was something that took place among unsupervised kids who had a lot of idle time on their hands. They say that an idle mind is the devil's playground. You now know what occurred from our idle time.

To every parent, be aware of your children's environment. I'm not telling you to be paranoid, but I am asking you to make sure you are careful when leaving your children unattended around other kids, especially those who are older. As children we all get curious, but sometimes in the midst of curiosity trouble is lingering. Parents please take the time and talk to your children about someone touching them in an improper manner. Explain to them the types of behaviors that are appropriate and inappropriate. These conversations may be uncomfortable, but which would you rather have for your child—an uncomfortable conversation that warns them of what improper conduct is or a child who grows into a resentful adult that hates him or herself, due to things that happened to them secretly?

PS Be on guard!

4

Masturbation

THE DAY WE MET seemed like one of the best days of my life. I was head over heels for you. Every time I thought about us touching, my eyes would get starry. I met you at such a young age and we continued our relationship well into my early thirties. Our first encounter had me chasing you down, and I wanted more!

Picture a kid tasting chocolate candy for the first time. The look of enjoyment on their face from the taste immediately lets you know that they're hooked, and so was I. I loved the feeling you gave me. You were my drug and I was definitely addicted. I made sure that we met up almost every day. This was our little secret because I knew others wouldn't understand, and plus it would have been embarrassing to share. So, I remained quiet and kept our affair under wraps. I had to be very careful when we met up, especially when I was younger and in the house with my family. I couldn't let anyone hear us playing around, so I had to learn how to enjoy you in silence. Once I got older and away from other people's ear shot, I was able to let you know just how much I enjoyed your company. You might as well have been my boyfriend because we stayed cuddled up. I was so used to us meeting that when I had someone in my life and we were sexually active, I didn't worry too much about them pleasing me because I had you. If need be, I knew you would take care of me.

In my younger years, I would lock myself in the bathroom or bedroom and stay for hours touching and rubbing until I felt this great sensation in my vagina. I really didn't know what I was doing, I just knew that it felt funny but good. As I got older, I knew exactly what to expect and how to make things happen. I was no longer the inexperienced little girl touching around trying to make it feel good. I had become a pro at self-gratification.

Actually, saying this out loud sounds crazy! How many of us would be proud to tell our friends that we masturbate? There you are, out to lunch and everyone is talking about what they did last night, and you respond with, "I didn't do much, I just masturbated." Sounds crazy, right? That's why those of us who did it, or still are participating in it, don't speak on it because somewhere on the inside we know that it's wrong.

Most of the time when I touched myself, I was either feeling horny, alone, or just bored. This was my way of feeling better. Once I got past how I was feeling, I was back to my norm and able to chill, but if I felt those unwarranted feelings come back, what do you think I did? You're absolutely right. I masturbated again. This had become such a routine that I started realizing it took more for me to reach a climax. Because of this, I had to open myself up to other things. It's like a person who starts doing drugs. They believe that what they start out doing is enough and that they'll never graduate to another level of being high. But once your body becomes accustomed to something, the only way to get to that next level of high you crave is to take it up a notch, and that's what I did.

> It's something how you can start a thing believing there is nothing wrong with it, and the next thing you know, you're involved in all sorts of stuff.

I started watching porn and while watching, I immediately felt the need to touch myself, but this experience was different. As I continued to watch, I began visualizing myself being touched by random people. This was that next level high I was talking about. I had allowed my mind to go to another realm to reach that sexual peak that I chased. At first it was a little weird thinking about people I didn't know touching me, but because of the feeling I got from it, I was all in. When I was in the moment, I couldn't have cared less about the nasty thoughts I was having, but after I was finished, I felt a little awkward.

What did I just open myself up to? I shrugged it off and kept it moving, but as you know, every time after that, I had to open myself up to the same magnitude to release. I was so open from watching porn that I started going to video stores, sneaking into the porn section to find videos to help me have an orgasm. After I would find the tape of choice, I'd go home and prepare myself for the unknown person that would be taking me to the next level of euphoria. At this point, you can rightfully say that I was in love with masturbation. It had gotten so bad that when I didn't have the movies, I had to think of being intimate with old boyfriends, dudes I was attracted to, or random people in order for me to have an orgasm. Whatever it was going to take to get me to that point, I did it. I was chasing masturbation like a heroin addict chases that first-time high. I know it sounds like I'm exaggerating, but if you only knew how stuck I was. No longer was this just a physical act, it was mental. I mentally would take myself places that caused my body to respond in the physical. By me opening up a door to invite others in while I masturbated, every time I touched myself, people always came to mind. There were times when I tried to close them out, but it didn't feel the same. I wanted the highest part of the high, not just a buzz, so I had to let them back in to get what I wanted. This feeling was now controlling me! Any time I felt a twinge in my lower pelvic area, I masturbated. What started off as a few touches here and there, had now made me its slave. I was completely enamored!

I know this may be a little deep for some, but because someone may be struggling with the same issue, transparency is a must.

Being that my transparency may become some people's "tea" time, I give you full permission to have your conversations to discuss what I've shared. But as you sip and converse back and forth, don't forget to tell people that I'm free, completely free from masturbating. Tell them that God delivered me and that I'm no longer bound. *I'm free. Are you?*

I wanna make sure I'm being completely honest. Please understand that there are moments when an urge may come and try to get me to fall back into what I'm feeling, but I don't succumb to it anymore. I've learned that just because I get an urge doesn't mean I have to submit. My body no longer controls me. I won't lie and say there weren't times, early on, that I didn't give into what I felt, because I did. But it wasn't the same. I felt dirty and regretted what had taken place. I wish I could've taken back the moment but since I couldn't, it made me determined not let it happen again.

Masturbation had now become something that I saw as self-violation. Viewing it this way made me keep my hands off of myself. When I think of being violated by someone, which I have, it makes me enraged and ready to go to war. So, if I feel that strongly about someone else touching and criminally violating me, why would I continue to do the same to myself?

Something to ponder on.

#Who'sYourMastur/Master???

5

Promiscuity

POPULARITY HAS BECOME my portion, and I am fascinated by it. I'm in my glory. Not for one second did I ever think that I would become a hot commodity. I knew what it was like to be popular in my community and in school because I was the class clown, the life of the party. But the popularity I craved was from the boys. I wanted them to want me. There were some guys who did like me, but there were others whose attention I didn't have, and it bothered me. Why? Because them not paying me any attention made me think that I wasn't pretty enough. Then one day the tables turned. The girl who was once rejected has now become the main attraction.

What is it about me that has finally grabbed the attention of the dudes I desired so badly? Is it my singing? Is it my dancing? Or was it something else? My talent did capture the attention of others, but there was one secret talent that many didn't know of, but some did gain the privilege of receiving an invitation ... Sex!

This had become a major ordeal in my life. It wasn't something that I did with just any and everybody, but I did share myself more than I'd like to admit. Even though I wasn't big on having sex, I sometimes found myself in some real compromising situations that made me feel like I couldn't say no. Being that I had the guy that every girl wanted on top of me, I couldn't shut down now. I felt like I had to keep quiet about how I truly felt, because had I spoke up, they may have walked away if we stopped having sex.

My Inner Thoughts

Is popularity really worth me feeling horrible about myself? (Somebody, please help me gather my thoughts.) Maybe I shouldn't entertain their conversations, but my ego oftentimes got in the way. The word among the guys I slept with was, "Pamela has that goodie-goodie!" And if you haven't guessed it by now, those words went straight to my head. #Pride

These words empowered me and made me feel like I was on top of the world. So, I had to live up to what was being said, even though it wasn't my preference. It wasn't the sex that made me feel good because most of the time it was terrible. It was the sense of being wanted that gave me satisfaction.

Just thinking they cared seemed to be enough for me to go through with the act that I many times dreaded. I was lying to myself, but what was I supposed to do. Even with some of the "cute guys" becoming my boyfriend and girls wanting to be in my position, popularity had let me down. It wasn't strong enough to make me whole, but I chose to stay in it anyway, because I was too weak to walk away and live what I deemed as regular.

> Before I go in any further, I want to make something clear. Every dude didn't get an opportunity to ride. I was selective. Your girl wasn't a ho, I just acted like one. Being that I was severely broken, I allowed myself to settle. And due to me settling, I gave up something so precious—my body.

To all my sister's reading this, I wanna share some advice with you. If he can't sport you on his arm and put a ring on your finger, don't become an easy lay and find yourself rolling in his sheets. You are a wife, not a ho!

Hiding My True Heart

I was the kind of girl who played around with dude's hearts, minds, and bodies if given the chance. To protect myself from being hurt, I would downplay my feelings like the dude meant nothing, just in case they didn't want to be involved with me any longer. I had to stay ready.

My perception of myself was so low that I felt the need to always be ahead of the game, just in case I got tossed to the side, so I would be dating one guy and talking to someone else on the side.

Even though I hated the situations I found myself in, I honestly loved the fact that all the attention was on me. What I desired was now in full effect. My thoughts were, *Who cares that this may be momentary? I was the center of attention and that's what matters most!* I was lying to myself. I wanted those I really cared for to love me, but I couldn't concentrate on that. This was not the premise of how we got together. They knew me because of what I gave them sexually, and what I gave had them coming back for more. This was not the time to get emotional. My mind was all over the place. I started having mixed emotions about what I was doing. I tried to convince myself that I was okay with doing the things I was doing.

I'll just keep this to myself and I won't tell anyone what I got going on. I'll keep this on the low!

I'm so glad that people didn't know how I moved back then because had they known they probably would have talked about me. Your girl may have been labeled as a ho, and that would have definitely led to fighting. No woman wants to be called out by her name, but if the shoe fits... wear it! Dear God, how can I get from under this? Literally!

This was becoming too much, but I had to keep my spot secured, so the fiasco continued.

I remember being with certain dudes and in my mind, I wanted *out*! It felt so nasty being touched by them but because of my lack of self-respect, I kept the party going. *Dang it*! I really wanted to do something else. I wanted something real. I was tired of being sexed! I didn't want to be touched on anymore, but it was so much a part of me that I no longer felt I could separate myself from it even if I tried.

The thoughts of the hands that have touched my bare skin makes me cringe. The look of disgust is not just on my face but felt inside my belly. How do I begin to say no to what others have become accustomed too?

Just like waking up in the morning, sex had become common. It was something that I did to maintain what I desired. I was now popular among the guys, but I was miserable. Wow!

Was popularity really cracked up to be all that I thought? It wasn't! It cost me my dignity and so much more, but I couldn't let go as of yet *because if I let it go, what happens to me? What am I supposed to do with being rejected? Ah, I am so torn.* What should be an easy decision is more complicated than I thought.

I made the decision to put myself out there in this way, and because I didn't have the confidence to show these guys my true heart, I opted and gave them the occasion to ride on top and on the back of me. And because I did so, they didn't come to know me as the nice girl. They knew me by the sex we had, and taking that away might have been a game changer for them.

I extended myself to multiple guys trying to fill voids they could never satisfy. The more sex I had, the more dejected and depressed I felt. I wanted more but I knew some of them didn't, so why play myself and act like it was more than just sex for me? I played the hand that I pretty much dealt myself and there was no one to blame accept me. So, unfortunately, I sat back and watched the cards fall wherever they hit the table. If they wanted to date, cool, and if they didn't, I had to pretend that I felt the same.

Then God intervened. Jesus Christ, the Son of God, began to show and tell me how special I was. His love didn't take advantage of me. It was intimate but sex was not required. All He wanted was my heart. He began to love me through my hurt even while I was still doing wrong. One day a light bulb went off, and I realized that I was being pimped by promiscuity. And on that day, I pulled up my panties and declared, "NO MORE!" I was no longer going to be a hole for dudes to sink into. I finally understand that I have value.

Hey promiscuity, can you hear me?

#We'reFinished!

6

Young Love

YOU WERE SHORT, brown-skinned, with wavy hair, dimples, and a great smile. Everything that a girl my age went for. You had the right requirements for teenage love. I thought you were such a cutie pie, but I never said anything about it. As a matter of fact, I never told anyone about my thoughts of you. There were so many people telling me how much you liked me, *even your mom*, but I wasn't beat. She and I had a huge laugh about your major crush on me, but after the laugh, I didn't think twice about it. Not until I noticed something different about you.

Many times, when I walked through the neighborhood, I'd see you with your friends and once you glanced over and saw me, you would jump on your bike, frantically, and ride off. You did this almost every time I saw you. I started feeling bad. I was like, *Aw, this is so cute. He really is crushing on you, P-girl.* You were so scared around me. Even though I felt bad, there was no way you could ever have the potential of being my boyfriend. You were a kid to me. If anything, you were more in the brother or cousin category, *but a boyfriend?* Not at all. Being that you liked me so much, I decided to be your friend. I thought that maybe by us being friends, you'd stop running away every time you saw me. *Boy was I wrong.* You still ran, but not as much. I never paid too much attention to you, but one day I saw this look on your face that hit my teenage heart. It made me smile, and I thought it was so sweet. But being who I was, I shook it off and kept it moving. I had my days when I wanted to saywe were a couple, but I knew better. *Why am I thinking of this little boy like this? Get it together, Pamela. This is certainly not the move you want to make.*

Now that I'm thinking clearly and I've gathered my thoughts, here you come *again* riding on your bike, but this time you do something different. I'm waiting on you to make eye contact so that you can take off in the other direction, but you smile and wave hello and breeze right by.

I was shocked! I was expecting you to do the norm and you didn't. It made me be like, *What?* So, I waved and smiled back while you pedaled away. This was so corny and childish, but for some odd reason, it caught a piece of my attention. I don't know if it was because you showed no fear, but something made me go *hmmm.* Like I said earlier, I had no interest in you, but something started happening.

When you weren't around, I found myself looking for you. *What am I thinking? He is too young and that ain't what I'm into. You liking me is cute, but that's about it.* Although I reminded and convinced myself of all these things that were true, I still kind of secretly liked you. *Eww! I don't want to like you. You're too young!* As I go back and forth in my head. I have to conclude that I do like you, and I'm ashamed of myself for feeling this way. Let me go hang out with some friends my age so that I can stop tripping.

There were times while hanging with my crew when I would see you, and I'd want to switch gears and come over to you but I couldn't.

Oh shoot, you just rode past on your bike. How can I see where you went, without it being obvious? As I walked through the neighborhood, there you were playing and having fun with your friends. I had to make sure you saw me, so I began to make myself noticeable in a way that would catch your attention. Once I got it, I would say hello and walk by.

I was ready to ditch my friends so I could come and hang around where you were, but I had to play it cool. I knew you would eventually make your way over to me, so I waited until you did. To be completely transparent. I really liked you a lot, and when I was around you, I had so much fun. I'm a little numerous about what I just said, because once people get to the end of this chapter, they may think a little different of me, but it is what it is.

There were times when I'd allow myself to be a kid. I remember how we would play at the playground by your house. We played freeze tag, I rode the merry-go-round until I felt sick and dizzy enough to throw up, and you even rode me on your bike. Thinking back on moments like these makes me smile because they were precious and pure. However, not being able to share with my homies about my new crush sucked. As a teenage girl, you always share with your homies who you have eyes for, but not this time. You were capturing my young heart and I had to keep it to my lonesome, because they wouldn't understand. Heck, I really didn't understand what was happening, but something was transpiring.

By spending time with you, I started really entertaining the thoughts of you liking me. *Nah! I can't likc him. Don't go there. Get your thoughts together, baby girl. You are almost a grown woman compared to him. You drink, you've had sex before, you cuss, and you're a teenager. It's cute and all but that's all it is. Leave it alone.* I told myself this was a no-no situation and I was cool with that but your family, every time I saw them, kept reminding me of the stupid crush you had on me. I know they were only telling me out of fun, but when I heard it, it made me think about being your girl. *This is crazy! I have to stop coming around because I'm starting to really wanna be with you.* Even though I knew it couldn't be, I loved how special I felt. You liking me had my head going in circles.

Here I am again, back in the same place trying to convince myself that we are only friends and that I'll see you whenever I see you. But that didn't work at all. I saw you almost once a day. I would come by your house just to sit and talk with you, but our conversations were close to none. You didn't know how to hold a conversation with me. *I should have known we had nothing in common. This is dumb of me! Why won't I just walk away? I'm so confused.*

There is one conversation I remember very vividly. That was the day you asked me for a kiss. I believe your little friends put you up to it because you didn't normally talk like that. Even though I thought it was cute, I knew there was no way I was putting my lips on yours. When I told you no, I saw that it smashed your little dream and I felt bad for you, but I was not changing my mind. I won't say that kissing you never crossed my mind, but there was something in me that knew that kissing you was not a good look.

I am so glad that nothing ever went down between

us. *Thank God*! The only things we ever did were talk, laugh, and hold hands *sometimes*. You bought me ice cream and I rode your bicycle a few times, and that was IT! Anything other than that was not in the plans. I believe me liking you had a lot to do with how you showed me so much attention.

Your interest in me was so innocent and pure that it made me want more. You had no motive, and that's what drew me in. Had you been older, I would have dated you in a heartbeat, but because of your age, I had to make sure certain boundaries weren't crossed.

I was a fourteen-year-old girl being pursued by a nine-year-old boy who made her feel special. Before meeting you I never experienced *from a boy* what being special felt like. This was all new. All I ever received from guys was them having a one-track mind when it came to me. And that was sex, sex, sex.

For you as a young boy to show me, *a damaged teenaged girl*, attention and motive-free interest made it hard for me to walk away. I am so thankful that even though it was difficult, I knew how to pump my brakes and not take advantage of you.

This is hard to write about without me feeling some kind of way because this was supposed to be my secret to the grave! Although me speaking out about you may raise a few eyebrows, I decided that if I'm going to tell my story, I have to say everything! When I think back on how misused I was, opening up about you becomes more freeing than embarrassing. All I ever wanted was to feel loved, and in your own little way, you expressed love to me at the age of nine. You *as a young boy* gave me your heart with no strings attached. Not one time did you ever try to hurt me. That's deep! I never had that revelation until now.

My Final Thoughts

According to statistics, they say that a child who has been molested at a young age more than likely has a chance of committing the same crime. I beg to differ! Statistics may have their numbers, but I had and have Jesus! And because of Him, I am nothing like my violator. If anything, I am the complete opposite, and it's only by the grace of God.

Because of all I've been through, I believe it's one of the main reasons why I love and protect kids as much as I do, especially my nieces and nephews.

To my young love, thank you for unknowingly helping and mending a young, hurting heart. God bless you always.

7

Mommy, Not Mommy

My Awakening

WHAT HAVE I DONE? I can't believe I did this to you! What was I thinking? At this particular time in my life, I was very selfish and into myself. You should be here right now. All three of you. Not for one second did I ever stop and think about the pain you may have felt being snatched from my womb. I only thought of myself and what I believed was best for me. I never even considered your feelings. You didn't ask to be a part of this world, but my choices brought you here, and due to my selfish behavior, I treated you as if you had no worth. When I look back on this, it sometimes causes my heart to hurt because the last thing I would ever want to do is hurt my babies.

It all began at the age of fifteen. I was having unprotected sex with my boyfriend and one day, I stopped getting my period. I knew something was up, but I wasn't expecting it to be the big shebang! At this time in my life I honestly wanted to have a baby. I had recently found out a friend of mine was pregnant, so I wanted to be pregnant too. This was insane. I had no clue nor understanding that a baby was nothing like having a baby doll.

I hid the fact that I hadn't gotten my period for as long as I could and then one day my mom asked the big question, "Are you pregnant?" I began to cry and started pleading my case. "No!" But little did I know she had found the letter I wrote to my friend saying that I thought I was. My mom made me a doctor's appointment and you guessed it right—I was with child. Because I was so young, my mom, although distraught over the entire situation, thought it would be best if I had an abortion.

In the midst of the decision-making, I didn't know how to feel. On one hand, I wanted to have my baby but on the other hand, there was an issue that was leading me to have doubts. I had second thoughts because I'd slept with my boyfriend's cousin twice. They were distant cousins but still family. I slept with him when my boyfriend and I broke up, but we quickly got back together. And now I had this situation, *a baby.* I honestly was a little relieved about the abortion because I wasn't going to have to tell my boyfriend I slept with his cousin, and I wouldn't have to worry about him not being the father. This was a lot for a fifteen-year-old to have to shoulder, but I did.

My boyfriend at the time knew I was pregnant, but he didn't know this part of the story. *Surprise.*

Baby number two happened a year later, and this time my mom was boiling mad. I was dating this guy that I was head over heels for, and I believe it was the first time that we laid and played, I got pregnant. *Dang it!* A few months went by and I noticed the same symptoms that went on during the first pregnancy were happening again. *Oh my goodness! What am I going to do?* I didn't want my boyfriend to catch on to me possibly being pregnant because I thought he would deny being the father, since we'd only been together for a month or so. I had to keep this on the low, especially from my mom. So I began faking like I was getting my period. I would make sure that I wasn't sexually active with my boyfriend for the days that my period should have been on. And I had a plan to execute in my house to keep all this under wraps. I would take clean maxi pads and roll them up in tissue and place them in the bathroom trash so my mom would think

I was getting my menstrual. How many of y'all know my mama was smarter than that?

One day out of the blue, my mom tells me that my aunt is taking me to the doctors. *Ahhh man! Here we go.* My aunt and I get to the doctors, and while I'm being examined, the doctor says, "You're pregnant again." My aunt, who knew nothing of my first pregnancy, blurts out, "Again?" I begin to cry, and while my aunt consoles me, she says, "I'm going to leave it up to you to tell your mom the truth." I tell her through my tears, "I'm going to speak with her." I wasn't planning on telling my mom anything. I just wanted my aunt to leave me alone.

A few weeks went by and my mom came to me and said, "Is there something you forgot to tell me?" I looked her in the face and said, "No." She then began to explain how she'd just talked to my aunt and my aunt asked her if Pammie talked to her about what happened at the doctor's. I looked at her with this stupid look on my face and she went haywire. She said, "I can't believe that you put yourself in the same situation." The tears ran down my face as she asked me, "What are you going to do?" This time around I wanted to keep the baby, I really did. But I knew the guy I was with would never believe it was his. He was a year younger than I was, and I knew he wasn't thinking about fatherhood.

I also had a small dilemma with this pregnancy as well. I was sleeping with my ex every once in a while, as well as with my new boo. This happened in the beginning of us getting to know each other, but when we committed, I left ole boy, *my ex,* alone. I had another sticky situation on my hands and opted for the abortion.

I finally got it together—no more pregnancies. *Yes!* Even though I was still having unprotected sex, I was being what they call "careful." Being that I knew the guy and we had history together, I didn't have to concern myself with him wearing a condom. At first, we started off with it, but it wasn't what either of us wanted, so we agreed that we knew each other enough to get our freak on and he wouldn't forget to pull out.

In this season of my life, my career had just started booming, so I knew I had to be extra careful because of my being what I was nicknamed— "Fertile Myrtle"—quick to get pregnant. We made it a thing and noted when to withdraw and how timing was everything. That's how serious we were about not complicating things.

More and more, I found myself sleeping with him because we had no strings attached. We did all that we could to be safe. There were a few close calls, but for the most part we were good. Then one day we must have drank too much alcohol, because we got sloppy. All this time we hadn't encountered any hiccups and then what happened? Pregnant. Here I was, twenty-two years old and definitely not looking to be a mommy. I was at a very pivotal point in my life and I wasn't about to slow down. *If I have a baby right now, my career may be over. They not going to wait for me to drop this load. I'm having an abortion!* This time around I didn't need anyone to tell me what to do. I had my mind made up and I was moving forward with my plans.

While making what I felt was the best decision for me, something strange occurred. The dude I was pregnant by begged me not to have an abortion. I knew he wasn't saying this because I was now famous, but because he really loved me and wanted to love his child. He didn't believe in abortions. But I wasn't trying to hear anything that he said. I had to do what was best for my career. *Did you catch that*? If I had to do what was best for my career, why would I put myself in such a situation? I told him that my decision was final, and he cried. He was so upset with me. I won't lie and say I didn't have thoughts about keeping my baby, but I couldn't slow things down now. I had to keep focused and shake it off. This time when I went through with the abortion, there was a little guilt that I felt; nonetheless, I kept it moving.

When I look back on this part of my life, I can't believe the depth of selfishness I had in my heart. I believe one of the most precious names a woman can be called is Mommy. I was given the opportunity three times and I turned away from it. To be a mom is such an amazing joy to me. It is one of my deepest desires once I'm married. I now know that it is a privilege to be a mother. To know that I gave up such an honor, three times, sometimes still affects me.

When it finally hit me as to what I did to my kids. I cried out to God and asked Him to forgive me for aborting the babies he gave and entrusted to me. I knew my heart was changed because I no longer could think of ever having another abortion. Had I known then what I know now, people would see that I have children instead of thinking that I don't.

Another reason why I no longer believe in abortion is because God has a plan for every child before they're inside the womb. Who am I and what have I created? Who am I to try and stop his plans? *I am not God!* Their life-span could have been for a hundred seconds or a hundred years. Who was I to decide that they shouldn't have experienced it?

Today, I look forward to becoming a mom. I can't wait to hear the sound of little feet running through the house laughing, playing, and calling me that beautiful name—Mommy. I know my history reeks of me being irresponsible when it comes to being pregnant, but my heart has been changed. I now know the beauty of being with child. I also have been preparing by practicing on my nieces, nephews, and godchildren, whom I love dearly.

There are two things I want to do before ending this chapter. I want to apologize to my babies that I aborted. I am so sorry for hurting you. I'm sorry I didn't recognize the beauty and value in you. I'm sorry I never gave you the chance to experience life, and I'm sorry that I was more concerned with me than I was for you. You didn't deserve what I allowed to become your fate. God called me to protect you and I didn't. Please forgive me. I know in my heart that all three of you are with God, and I pray one day I get to meet you face-to-face so that I can hug and kiss you. If I could turn back the hands of time, we would have never parted. I love you always. #HeavenBound

To the man/old boyfriend who was strong enough to tell me, at the age of twenty-two, that getting an abortion was wrong and how you didn't agree, t*hank you for not holding back your words.* Thank you for letting me know you weren't just going to agree with me, and that speaking your piece was a must. I also want to apologize for blowing you off as if you had no say with the pregnancy. I selfishly took your child away from you and I didn't even care to hear you out. I'm sorry for not considering your feelings. Back then I thought it was all about me, and it wasn't. I was a real jerk, and I'm sorry for how I treated you and our baby. I'm not sure of the extent of pain I caused you on that day, or many days after, but I ask you to forgive me for all of it. I didn't appreciate the beauty of life the way I do now. If I did, our baby would be alive. God bless you, your wife, and children, always.

#I'veBeenForgiven

8

HIV Scare

WHAT IN THE WORLD are you doing sitting at my kitchen table? Who let you in? There is no way you should be inside this house right now, especially if they knew our history. My brother would cut you at your knees! Why are you here and why now? After all these years, you really think it's cool to show up like this? I am so beside myself because I am completely caught off guard with this one. I don't mean to sound harsh, but we have nothing in common. All I can do is shake my head and try to understand what this popup visit is all about? *I've moved on!*

I was honestly gone after the first encounter but somehow you talked me into a second one, and after that we were done, *for real.* It was so stupid of me to let it go down twice, but that's neither here nor there. I don't know what you want but it ain't nothing, bruh. It's not like we had some type of relationship going. So, what's good?

Seeing a part of you at my kitchen table has me extremely infuriated, but I thank God that I know how to keep calm under pressure. *Don't let anybody see you sweat. You got this. Stay calm and put on that fake smile before your cover is blown.*

As my eyes roll and my head shakes from the annoyance of your presence, the feeling of disgust is unshakable. I want to scream out all types of cuss words, but I have to hold my composure. *This is not a good look. Dang it! You had no right showing up here like this. I gotta get rid of you quickly! Think Pamela!* I grab you up and dash out of the kitchen with you in hand, and off to my room we go, hoping that no one noticed. I get you upstairs without any questions, *thank God!*

The coast is clear, and it seems like no one is on to us, so I guess it's time to hear what you need to say. I rip you open and unfold what seems to be a lengthy letter. As I begin to read your words, my insides are curling up. Just hearing you say you miss me and how you remember what took place between us is making me sick. What made you contact me? *Ahhh!* I am so ticked off right now! Just because you got locked up doesn't mean I had to get a letter. Everything was going just fine and you just jacked my entire day up.

As I'm writing I ask myself, "What were you thinking? Why didn't you stick to no when he asked you? What made you sleep with him?" I really had to take a moment and tell God, thank you because I had no idea what was coming next. The outcome could have been fatal, but God!

Now let's get back to the letter, and it reads:

"I miss you. I miss sexing you and how it felt." *What did you just say to me? No, you didn't just say that. This is so nasty! First of all, the sex we had was whack and it was two times too many. But let me ask you this, "Was there something you forgot to mention? Did you leave out one huge detail?"* Yes, you did! *How about you forgot to tell me that you were sleeping with a woman who was HIV positive!*

I don't discriminate against anyone who is fighting with this disease; my heart goes out to them. But I'm just addressing you Mr. lover boy. Had I been aware of you sleeping with her, I would have kept my panties on my backside, *but I can't be upset with you without being upset with myself.* I didn't even want to sleep with you but being young and dumb I allowed your words to go to my head. You expressed how good it was going to be and pleaded with me. I became prideful and thought it was all about me and fell right into your trap. It was something that you said that sparked me into giving you some. It was when you made the statement about how you knew it was so good, *my ego went through the roof and my panties came off.* I just knew it was all about me because of how you were talking, but it was actually you getting what you wanted no matter how it made you sound. And to make matters worse our little escapade was unprotected. *My teenage arrogance could have been so costly.*

Being that we had experienced two unwanted encounters. I made sure to avoid you because I was sure I didn't want a third. After a while, I didn't have to avoid you anymore because you had gotten locked up. I heard your time was going to be long, so I was free to walk the streets again. You had become a part of my lost files. Never wanting to remember and hoping no one would ever find out what went down. But to my surprise I was about to run into something that would shake me to my core.

I began to hear people talk about a woman who was HIV positive that lived in our neighborhood, who I knew very well. It was really scary because this was the first time, I'd ever been that close to such a situation. It was the first talk of such in our little community. I remember when the dudes in our community began to discuss who did and who didn't sleep with her, and your name was called as one who did. My heart could have stopped! I could have died right where I was standing, but I had to play it off. I didn't mumble a word, but I was screaming on the inside. My head was spinning with fear. *What did they just say?* Wait, wait, wait! *Does he have HIV too? Do I have it? I'm young! This is not happening to me! What am I supposed to do?*

As I continued to read your letter knowing what I knew, it made me extremely upset and sick all at the same time. *Do I write back and cuss you out and tell you all that I know? Or do I ignore you and hope that you never write me again.* I chose the latter. I was so afraid to get tested, so I didn't, but it's something how God will make you face things.

Throughout the rest of my teenage years I had to get a lot of blood work done. HIV testing was one of the tests that I would take, and by the goodness of God it was, and still is to this day, negative. God blocked it!

Those were some of the most frightening years, but they taught me how to keep my panties on my backside. Until this day, I am one that practices abstinence. If I don't have a wedding ring on my finger, sex is not an option.

I remember the first time I saw you when you finally came home from jail. My stomach sank. Seeing you brought back so many emotions about what I went through mentally, and I didn't want you to speak about anything concerning our past. It felt so awkward, but I played it cool. We spoke briefly and I kept it moving. There were times when I looked into your eyes and it seemed as if you wanted me to remember what took place between us, but I gave no opportunity for that pointless conversation to come up. I was cordial and kept it moving.

I'll end by saying this. It's so important to never judge a book by its cover because who would have ever thought that HIV testing was a part of my story. It was only by God's mercy that neither he nor I contacted the disease. Pride and arrogance almost cost me my health and it could have taken my life. I was so prideful, thinking that my sex was the greatest. Not realizing that death was inches away.

#Something2thinkAbout...

9

The Wrong Attention

I'M NOT REALLY SURE how we have gotten to this place, but we are definitely out of pocket. To look into your face and see lust in your eyes is beyond chilling to me.

You believe that you have what? Have feelings for me? That is crazy! There is no way in the world that you could think that having feelings for me is right. Are you on something? Let's take a minute and assess who I am to you, because I believe that once you do that, you'll come back to reality and realize that you're tripping and out of line in your thought process.

I'm actually starting to become a little weirded out and scared when I'm around you, because at this point, I have no idea as to what you're capable of doing or what you're going to say.

You coming on to me really came from out of nowhere. Usually when something like this occurs the aggressor may tend to flirt a little here and there. They may even come with some sly remarks to see if the person they are pursuing will bite, but you showed no signs of such. I remember one day you were talking to me regular and then the next few times I saw you, you were trying to press your body up against me and rub my leg.

I never gave you the impression that this was okay, but I also never told you to stop. In my head I was yelling, "Leave me alone!" But for whatever reason my mouth wouldn't open up to express what my mind so eagerly wanted to say. As you stood in front of me trying to talk me into kissing you, I quickly understood that there was something deeper going on with you. You had this crazed look in your eyes that alarmed me, and I knew that you had mentally checked out. Your sense of reality had taken a back seat and your Rico Suave conversation was in full effect. I couldn't wait for you to get out of my face because I wasn't interested in you, and plus, this was nasty and wrong. I appeased you by allowing you to get everything you needed to say off of your chest because I didn't want to upset you, and I was a little afraid of you due to your state of mind. Once you finished talking and your words came to an end, my next move was to get you out of my face so that I could high tail it in the opposite direction.

It was sickening hearing you say the things that you

said to me. You were telling me how cute I was, and how you liked me and wanted to be with me intimately. I never would have expected you of all people to step to me in such a foul manner. To be honest, most of your words on that particular day are still a blur. I was in so much disbelief about you approaching me that I couldn't really hear you, but I do remember the gross seductive look on your face.

In that moment I lost so much respect for you. You had become like everyone else who hurt me. You were no longer the one I looked up too. You now were just like one of the others that violated me, so when I saw you coming from afar, I would go in the opposite direction. I did everything I could to avoid you because I didn't want to battle with you trying to push up or play around with me.

Is this seriously happening?

This is not cool at all!

You are family!

Really???

There were guys who took advantage of me for years, but you were supposed to be different. I would never have thought that you would add to the hurt and shame I've previously endured. Every time I turned around someone that I trusted wanted to misuse me, and the clincher is … I let them! *I am so tired of this! Why does it seem as if every man that gets close to me has an ulterior motive*? Even with me feeling low, disrespected, and mistreated, I have to shamefully admit there was a part of me that started entertaining your passes. I was low key waiting to hear what you had to say. This was so unhealthy. *How am I liking and hating something at the same time? Why are you coming on to me and why am I putting up with it?* This had to be the most disturbing feeling in the world, but yet and still, I hadn't shut you down. This was nasty and dead wrong. I wanted you to stop but I didn't know how to say it. I had become so accustomed to being the girl that guys thought it was okay to mistreat that I didn't know how to stand up for myself at all.

At this point I was completely confused, and I didn't know what to do. Thinking back to those private talks we had makes my skin crawl. I was saying things to you that I had no intention of ever fulfilling, and you were saying things to me that you would have been more than happy to fulfill, if given the opportunity. But I wasn't down with the get down. I was just a slick talker who loved the fact that someone was thinking of me.

I recall the day when I started talking really inappropriately to you. I was telling you how I would put my hands in your pants and rub on your dick, among other things that would arouse you. My words were becoming as lewd as yours. You made it clear that sexing me was what you wanted and making me your girl was the goal. The more vulgar my words became, the more you wanted to get at me. I was all talk, never desiring to ever put things into action. It was something about being noticed that I craved.

I'm so thankful that when these words were being exchanged that we weren't face-to-face because it could have gotten even more ugly than what it already was. I only spoke what I thought you wanted to hear, and by me talking to you in such a provocative way, it made you come at me even harder. I wanted this nonsense to stop because I knew in my heart that it was wrong. *What if someone finds out what you and I have been saying to one another?* It would have been terrible. Even with me telling myself that I wanted it to stop, it still continued, but only when you initiated the conversation. *What the heck is wrong with me? Why am I allowing this to go on?* There had to be something deeper lurking in the background of all of this because I really didn't want these conversations to go on, but almost every time, I found myself indulging. Afterward I would feel so horrible that I wanted to hide. I wished that it could all just go away and we could act as if none of this ever happened, but that wasn't the case.

As I got older and began to examine myself, I wanted to know why I entertained your unwanted conversations. What was driving me to put up with the very thing I wanted to avoid? What was holding me there?

And one day the truth revealed itself. It was my secret thirst for attention. I craved it, I wanted it, and I even believed that I needed it. I wanted someone to notice and yearn for me. I'm not talking about attention in a sexual way but in an "I love you and want to hug you" type of way. I wanted to hear that I was beautiful and that I was special, but I didn't receive that, so I chose what was in front of me, even at the cost of me feeling degraded. I desired more for myself, but because I was so use to being treated badly, this was a part of my norm. I allowed myself to be devalued because of the lack of love I had for myself.

It stings to openly share that I was an attention whore and that I allowed myself to be cheapened for the sake of it. I dare not try to place all the blame on you because I also knew better. I, too, played a major part in what went on. I should have never entertained your words and flirted back with you when you came at me with the craziness. But due to my selfish need of attention, I opened up an unwanted door that was hard to close.

One thing I can say with my head looking up to the sky is, we never kissed or slept together. I wasn't thinking or looking for that to ever come to pass, nor did I ever desire for it to be. What I won't do is lessen the fact of what I allowed and partook in. This was distasteful and very unsuitable, especially for family. Looking back, I was the one who opened up the door and gave you access to me. You would have never gotten in had I'd been confident in who I was, but my insecurities welcomed you even though I was fully aware that your intent was poisonous. My deep, dark displeasure of myself didn't discriminate on whom or what comforted it. That inward starvation for attention cried out and because of it being a stronghold in my life at the time, it got fed with just what it wanted!

> To the man I called "cuz," I'm not sure if you ever think back to this time. God knows I sure didn't want to go back, but I've learned that it's the only way to go forward. I want to openly apologize for leading you on back then. We were young, well I was, but we were both old enough to know right from wrong. Being that I didn't shut down our gross conversations, it caused me to not want to hear from you, due to fear of what would come from your mouth. It also caused you to think I was a tease and playing hard to get, which actually made you even more pursuant, when all I truly wanted was for you to leave me alone.

I'm not going to go on a rant, but I hope you haven't tried to erase what went down between the two of us by blanking it out of your mind, *like I tried to do*, and make it seem as if it never happened. If you did, it's time to deal with the reality of how wrong our actions were, and no longer pretend that this is just something regular that happens between family. It's time to take full ownership for this ugly secret and remove its lingering stench from the atmosphere.

I finally can say goodbye to this segment of my life that held my lips bound together because of the shame of my actions. But today I know that someone has been waiting for me to be un-muted, so I speak. My quiet thoughts that once frightened me are now under my feet. I am a new creation in Christ.

My hope is that the person who has or is struggling with such an issue would gain strength from my words. Please remember,

#there is hope for the weary.

10

Le Toilet

FLUSH. This was a familiar sound that I unfortunately knew very well. The reason why is because for most of my life, all I ever did was consume people's waste. For years, I allowed myself to be a place for people's dumping. I never realized that I was functioning like a toilet.

A toilet is a fixed receptacle into which a person may urinate or defecate. Its job is to catch and receive waste, and once received, the person who has emptied themselves out gets up, pulls up their pants, flushes *well some don't even have the audacity to flush*, washes their hands, then leaves. There is no other use a toilet has but to accept, and expel, whatever it is given. I've swallowed and endured so much stuff from people that it ain't even funny. So many of them have never even thought to look back. *Smh.* But those who did eventually look back, their only reason for doing so was only to dump on me again. *That's so foul to me. It makes me angry when I think of this. Why wouldn't I say anything?*

The only thing that separated me from a porcelain toilet was that I could talk. I had become so immune to being a dumping place that it was now engrafted into my nature. Because I didn't open my mouth to speak, I gave people the authority to sit upon the throne of my life and poop all over me.

There I was, left with trying to digest the hurt I felt. I was so tired of being the go-to person, *and I mean I was that for almost everybody.* Who could I run to in my time of desperation and need? But I can't blame them for everything because I was the one who made myself susceptible to swallowing whatever they dropped on me, whether it was big or small. And because I chose to eat it, there I was left alone trying to figure out a way to flush my soul, while those same people went on with their lives living guilt free. *Why in the world would I take such a posture?* It behooves me to admit that I permitted such things, but I finally realized why I wouldn't speak up. I didn't speak up because I didn't want to be alone. I wanted people to like me even though I didn't like what was being done to me. I had become just like that porcelain toilet, still, cold and ready for a dumping.

It's hard to admit and identify myself with such an ugly truth, but there is no other way for

> deliverance. The stench of defeat and purposeless living reeked from my being. All I knew to do was to take the cards I was dealt, even when I knew the hand was rigged. The person dealing the cards knew exactly how they were setting things up, and honestly, sometimes I knew as well but still decided to play.

There are so many people, that I now know of by God's revealing, who maliciously set out to gain my trust. It's sad, but true. Once they gained my trust, I opened up and shared my brokenness, which in turn gave them access on how to get what they wanted from me. My sharing caused them to garner insight on what words to use on me to pull at the strings of my heart. And when they were pulled, it would either make me feel guilty to help, or emotional to give.

Let me paint this picture for you real quick. Envision yourself going into a bathroom and when you walk inside you find that the toilet hasn't been flushed. Your face immediately becomes screwed up. You're boiling mad and you want to cuss but you start praying, because that is godlike. Just the sight of it has you ticked off beyond words, and let's not forget there are different levels to what you may have walked into. It could have been a number one, a number two, *sounds like I'm about to order from McDonald's* or something worse, like a number three with the addition of blood. *I'm done. I'm bothered by just writing it.*

Who wants to see something that came out of someone else? Sometimes I don't want to see the stuff that comes out of me, never mind someone else.

My reason for painting such a graphic visual is because I was once that messy toilet. Everything that was ever dumped in or on me was now sitting at the surface of my life. This was exactly how I looked when I allowed dudes *I didn't want to sleep with,* to climb on top of me and dump themselves into me, which left me filled with their waste. Or how about my so-called friends who I really believed were friends, but only stuck around just to get what they could, because they knew Pamela had a big heart. They would dump their problems on me and sometimes even their bills, and what did I do? I received them as my own and paid them. Or just maybe I'm talking about the ones who said we were family for life, but they only made this claim to stay in close proximity to me because of what I could potentially do for them, or where they thought I could take them.

Close your eyes for a minute. Picture that toilet again. Do you see it? *There's something I forgot to mention.* A toilet has a sewage line, to rid itself of waste in the sewer when flushed. But as for me, who was going to flush me and help me rid myself of all the waste that was sitting within me? I was overflowing with dung.

Can you imagine the smell of a toilet that hasn't been flushed in years? *My face just frowned up the same way yours did.* It probably would have the most putrefying funk that ever hit your nose. You might even throw up from the sickening stench in the air. Well I can relate to such a funk. There was a smell that people began to get a whiff of that started exuding from my life, and that stench was anger. Due to me not having an outlet *a good flushing*, I had years upon years of things piled up inside that I sat with, and it caused me to become extremely angry. I carried around mounds of waste that weighed me down as I watched the people who dumped on me walk around light-footed without a care in the world, while I remained bogged down in heaviness without anyone to assist. Something had to give. Enough was enough!

As I came to this resolve I knew there were things I needed to confront, and those were the people who took advantage of me. First, I would like to let you all know I hold nothing in my heart against you, but please be advised that it stops here. No longer will you have the opportunity to dump your waste in, on, or around me. I hope the best for you, but today we part ways. No longer will you have access to my life. You may think you can manipulate the situation like you use to with tears, and/or your guilt trips that made me feel bad and caused me to re-embrace you, but that's dead. I'm letting go. As a matter of fact, I already have. I have to do what's best for me and you're no longer good for me. It's hard to even think of so many of you not being close to my side anymore, but I would rather you be gone than to use me with the wrong intent.

My Declaration

I, Pamela Long, no longer give people the permission to defile or misuse me. I've closed the door! I take back my dignity and honor, and I refuse to turn my face away from the truth I see in people anymore. I will believe what God shows me from the beginning so that I can avoid being dumped on. I am no longer a means of dumping. I finally know *and still am learning* my worth, and those who don't know what I now know about myself, *will be cut off.* This toilet is not only out of order, but it has been demo-ed.

#IFinallyKnowMyWorth

11

Girl Trouble

YO! WHAT ARE YOU DOING? Chill! What in the world is wrong with you? You don't need to drink no more because you are way out of character. I know that we have a lot of love for each other but for you to be trying to kiss me is crazy! Yo! Chill out! You are real drunk right now and you need to pull yourself together, because this is not the move. I didn't know you couldn't hold your liquor. *If I knew that*, we would have drunk some Kool-Aid or something. You are on a whole different level right now and I'm not going there with you, so chill!

I can't believe how you lunged at me and started wrestling with me on the floor for a kiss, but once you realized that I wasn't going to stop wrestling, you started apologizing. You told me how embarrassed you felt and that you never did anything like that before. You began to explain that you didn't know what it was that made you come at me the way you did, and how you were so sorry. As you were speaking, I sat there looking at you in awe. I couldn't believe that I just had to fight my friend off of me! *What in the world just happened? Who does this?*

In my head I was like, you need to go home, but outwardly I remained calm and let you finish talking. You then continued telling me that you never dealt with or felt this way about a female, and that you didn't know what it was that made you want to kiss me.

Thinking back on your actions that day makes me believe that you lied concerning that statement, but that's water under the bridge, so I digress. For a moment I became a little nervous because you seemed to be unstable and unpredictable, but as we continued to talk, I shrugged it off as you having too much to drink. The next day you apologized again for your behavior and I forgave you and that was the end of that, so I thought. I didn't know things were about to drastically change.

We now were closer than close, and every time someone saw me, they also saw you. We did almost everything together. You were my road dog and we stayed on the move. You were with me so much that when we came around, I saw the funny stares from some people, which made me uncomfortable, but I kept you around anyway. I felt uncomfortable because I could feel their quiet, inner conversations they had going on in their head about us. I wanted them to know that they were wrong, so in return I would say, "We ain't no couple, I don't date girls. I have a boyfriend, and plus, this ain't my cup of tea." Did you get that? Unfortunately, I never addressed them openly. I just hoped that they could feel or hear my internal thoughts in my head the same way I felt theirs.

I was so upset. I didn't want people believing false information about me. *Was there something about you that I didn't know? Did I miss something? I know you told me that you'd never been involved with a woman, but why is it that since I've been around you, people are thinking you're my girl.* This was something I should've given my attention to, but because I was always closing my eyes to the truth, I turned my face from it. I tried to make light of the truth that was staring me in my face, so I went with the flow and tried not to overthink stuff. *Wrong!*

Because of me not nipping things in the bud and letting you know if you ever came at me again in such a way that the outcome wouldn't be pretty, I left the door wide open for the opportunity for you to do it again. You were up to something and I was completely oblivious to your plan.

To be completely honest, I had a few things on my

mind as well that I kept quiet about in regards to what happened the night you came on to me. After it all went down, I thought about it a lot. As I thought about it, I became puffed up. I felt like I was the one that everybody wanted. Unbeknownst to you, I was beyond flattered. My ego and pride went through the roof. I just knew that I was "Miss Irresistible." Not only do the guys like sleeping with me, but now this girl wants me too. I quietly went back and forth in my head about letting you go down on me, but that's where it would end for me because I wasn't doing it back. I already planned things out about what was, and what wasn't going to occur. I made sure that I kept my little secret but as time went on, my little secret became a reality. I don't know what made me cave in, but I did. I told myself this was just a one-night thing. But that quickly turned into you saying just one more time, which eventually led to you calling me your girlfriend, and that's the word that freaked me out. It freaked me out because I was a girl, and girls don't have girlfriends, because if they do, they are considered gay. And I was not gay!

What am I doing? This has to stop. But I didn't want to walk away because it felt good, sexually. I knew I was tripping, but it was the climax that I enjoyed. There were times when I felt bad because I had a boyfriend, and he knew that we were "good friends." The two of you were also really cool with each other. Then, from out of nowhere, you began to get mad with me because I continued dating him. *We are not together! This was only one night that turned into something completely different. I can't help it if you're catching feelings for me because that wasn't a part of the plan. I'm not leaving him and hopefully you don't think I'll be leaving him for you. That ain't going down.*

We had our issues concerning him, and we finally got past the argument stages and agreed to disagree. And then from out of nowhere came a twist.

You were a beautiful young lady and I saw plenty of dudes trying to holler at you, but one day when I saw you flirt back, I became jealous. *Wait, wait, wait. Why am I so mad?* I was trying my best to hide it, but I couldn't hold it in, so I confronted you. We had a major blowup and I went off! You stood there at first looking perplexed, and then you began to argue back. Once things settled down, we agreed to you not talking to guys in front of me. Hold up! I thought I just said I didn't like girls, and that I wasn't supposed to be with a girl. *So why is it that I'm making some type of arrangement with her about what she will and will not do?*

Questions were now being asked more frequently about us. "Why are they always together? Are they friends or are they lovers?" To me, we were friends with benefits, but the longer I stayed involved with you, the more committed I became, unknowingly. Word had gotten back to my boyfriend that we were messing around, and he stood up for me telling people they were wrong, and that you and I were just friends. *He was so innocent in all of this.* I'm not sure if he didn't really see it or if he just didn't want to believe that I could do something like that to him. You, also, were getting to know his cousin who liked you, so that also could have thrown him off. I really had moments when I felt bad for him because he really cared about me, but at this point leaving the situation with you alone had become a little harder than what I thought. *How did I wind up in this place*?

Let's go back to the beginning.

I never expected us to do anything like this and it completely caught me off guard. It happened when I was around eight or nine years old. We were playing in the hallway upstairs at my house and for whatever reason we kissed. It was a few pecks, some squeezing of the butts, and then we went back to playing. I don't remember what exactly brought that on, but afterwards it was as if it never happened. After that encounter there were times when we stayed over each other's houses. When you and I slept in the bed together, we always ended up cuddling up under each other when we slept. There were a few times that we laid on top of each other and did a little pumping, but that was it. It seemed to be innocent, but now when I think back on it, the devil was setting me up. I can now see that his plan was for me to believe that I was gay, and he came for me at a young age.

> This is why it's so important to keep watch of children and to be careful as to what their little eyes see and what their ears hear, even while still in the womb. Children are oftentimes curious, and curious minds can lead to experimental activity, which has the potential to alter a child's future forever. Take heed from someone who knows firsthand.

When I was younger, a lot of people referred to me as a tomboy and because I didn't know any better, I embraced it. I liked climbing trees, running with the boys, playing sports, and anything else the boys could do. It wasn't because I desired to be a boy. I was just a tough little cookie who just so happened to be strong enough to take a hit and even a hard tackle while playing football with the fellows, or sliding in the dirt for home base while playing baseball. Playing with baby dolls, *which I also did,* was too easy. I was the kid who needed to be active. I had too much energy to sit still, and what the boys had going on was more exciting and competitive. I was just being me, but to others I was categorized as a tomboy. Nowhere in my DNA did I have the makeup or anatomy of a boy, but yet and still the word boy was attached to me. *It's something how words have the power to create. The mouth is such a powerful tool that if we are not careful, we can misuse it and become reckless with it, whether it's intentional or not.* Since there is death and life in the tongue, what we say can either help to build up or tear people down. No one ever knew how the word tomboy would subconsciously begin to shape my thinking of myself as I grew up. *I know I didn't.*

Never underestimate the power of your words. They are more powerful than you think. This is probably why God gave us one mouth because he knows the depths of what spoken words can do.

The older I got, the more run-ins I'd seem to have with girls. I didn't understand why, so I made sure I kept it hidden. I had crushes on two of my friends. I loved them and I knew they loved me, but something about my side of the love felt weird. I always told them how much I loved them, and I wanted them to know that I truly meant it. I remember when one of my friends, the one I really was attached to, went away on vacation. I felt lost without her. I had this unexplainable love for her that made me want to see her and spend all of my time with her. Maybe it was because she made me feel like she genuinely cared about me. The thing that I loved about my other friend was her beauty. She was gorgeous to me. I could have stared at her all day. *What is going on with me? This is different. Oh well, I just love my friends a lot! I'm good.*

I now know that a lot of it had to do with how I viewed myself. I always felt like the unwanted ugly duckling, and due to my lack of self-love, I viewed beauty only as an outward appearance rather than an inner attribute. Every time I would look at these two particular girls, I saw their beauty and I desired it. I thought if I couldn't be beautiful, at least I could somewhat have it by having these two girls in my inner circle. Everything I believed I wasn't helped and assisted me in gravitating to the beauty I saw in the faces of these young ladies. I never thought of them sexually, but I did want to protect them at every cost, and I also made sure I was always there for them no matter what. *I never told them I liked them, nor did we ever have any relations. This was something I kept to myself up until this very day.* All they knew was that Pam was a good friend and I would do anything for them. *My thought process was so jumbled up.* I would fight with myself saying, *What's going on with you, girl? Get these crazy thoughts out of your mind. You're buggin'! Girls are not supposed to like girls! Shake this mess off of you. Come on, Pamela! What are you thinking?*

And just when I thought I was passed that hump, something else arose. When I was fifteen an older woman approached me and began flirting with me. This chick said something to me in front of my homies and I was hot! I never gave her the impression that I liked her, or girls for that matter.

So off course I showed out a little bit, but deep down I was like *wow.* It was a "wow" moment for me because I felt like someone older was checking for me. The attention was cool when I was by myself, but if my friends were around, I was like "This lady is crazy." She and I never messed around, nor did we have moments of being alone. I just thought that her wanting to be with me was cool because it fed my emptiness of wanting to be wanted. After a while, it seemed like more and more females tried to get at me, but I wasn't with it. I had no interest in being intimate with a female. I just liked flirting with the attention. I really didn't want to get involved, but there is a saying that is so true. When you play with fire, you get burned. And my burning came around the age of twenty, going on twenty-one.

The very thing I said I didn't want, I now had on the low. Remember ole girl I was talking about in the beginning of the chapter? She was now my girlfriend. *What am I doing with a girlfriend? This cannot get out. I have to keep this hidden. I'm not supposed to have a girl. I'm a girl! You love me? This sounds crazy! What am I doing? I like playing around with you, but this talk about us being girlfriends is extreme.* In the infamous words of my brother, "What in the tarnation?"

Needless to say, we were on and off for a few years until finally things came to an end. *Yes, it's over! Finally, all of this is behind me and I can get back to my regular life.* I told myself before we broke up, that I was finished with this girl stuff. I was so serious. I wasn't into girls like that and I wasn't really about that life, and that's why I hid it. But little did I know, once you open up a door to something, it's not that easy to close it. The words that I uttered about not being with another woman led me to four other relationships. Playing and flirting around with women had become a part of me. It wasn't forthright because I didn't want or need that kind of attention, but I was checking for women just as much as dudes would. What I mean by that is, when I saw a woman I thought was nice looking, I did everything I could just to get a look at her. That was good enough for me. I wasn't trying to talk to every woman, but I sure did eye them.

There came a point when I could see in some women what others could not. I could see their curiosity of wanting to be with a woman, and I played into it. I played dumb when they would try to come on to me, or when they'd ask me if I liked women. For the most part it was the attention that I thrived on. Once my ego was fed, I was good. I wasn't that girl who was giving oral sex to anybody!

#Itwasnotgoingdown! Literally.

I had now embraced a lifestyle that I never thought I would. My thought pattern had changed. My words earlier on were, *This is not right, girls shouldn't have girlfriends.* But my words had changed to, *This woman thing ain't too bad, it's okay to be with her if you want to.* My entire posture had changed due to my involvement. There was a time when I had a different stance, but compromise had caused me to shift my thinking. It wasn't about trying to sex them because that was not my forte. I just wanted to see if I could get their attention. That was my goal. I had become so engulfed with the thought of women that my desire to have children with a man was obsolete. If I did sleep with a man, I told myself at the time, it would have only been for the pregnancy. I foolishly agreed with the female I was with at the time to raise children with her. *What in the world did I just say?* I really had moments of entertaining these twisted thoughts. I was all the way in this thing and didn't even realize how deep I had gone.

In the midst of me doing me, *as some would say,* there was always this part of me that wrestled with totally saying I was gay. That word was not for me. I wasn't going to be labeled. I wasn't even comfortable thinking that I was bisexual. *Was I just a freak who loved getting her rocks off, or was I a gay woman?* It angered me when I heard people say that I was gay. Why was I so offended? I now know the reason why. In my heart of hearts, I knew sleeping with a woman was wrong. I wanted to do what I wanted without the consequences and labels. I was not a homosexual nor was I a bisexual. I was a broken young woman who was looking for love from anyone who I thought showed it. I realized that any attention filled the gaps of my emptiness. Even when I knew it was wrong, I still went with it because I needed to feel something. Did I enjoy sleeping with women? Yes, I did. *I'm not going to water it down or lie.* But I also knew it was wrong and that made me uncomfortable. Even in my compromising of self, I was torn between living in a lie or turning to truth.

My battle with women was difficult to let go of because I had become used to being with a woman and her touch. This was definitely something I couldn't accomplish on my own. I needed help. I remember asking Jesus Christ to help me. I asked him to change my heart if it was wrong to lay with a woman. I didn't want to practice anything that wasn't pleasing in his sight any longer, and he did it. He loved me in and through the deliverance. I had to put the work in though. I studied the Scriptures, I prayed, I denied my body cravings, I cried, and sometimes I kicked and screamed. But I held fast to God's Word and He changed me.

God is able to change every man or woman if we desire to be changed. *Change comes to those who really want it. I am not only referring to homosexuality.* God is able to change the heart of any man or woman who has something going on in their lives that is contrary to his truth. *Did you catch that? His truth and not ours.* If you're a liar, a cheater, a thief, a person who overeats, etc.... God is able! He specializes in every area of life.

Please know that I am not bashing anyone, because I love everybody. There is just one thing I can't and won't play with and that's my accountability to God. I am accountable for telling the truth, even if the truth causes people to be upset with me. God is able to change all humanity if we are willing to let go and let him take over.

Before I end this chapter, I wanted to share this last thing. *I was still living in the same house with this woman when I gave my life to Christ.* Denying myself was not easy, but I wanted to know and live by God's truth regardless of how I felt. There were times when she wanted to be intimate and I had to say no. This caused many arguments, but I had to stand my ground. This wasn't just for me but for us. *I wanted her to be free too.* I won't lie and say there wasn't a time or two that I fell back into her arms in the process, because I would be lying. But I can say that I got back up determined to live in accordance to the Word of God, *and plus, it was no longer the same.* The times that I fell back into her arms, I was praying and asking God to forgive me, and desiring to be free from what I knew was a lie.

Today I am totally free! By the grace of God, I am and forever will be walking in my deliverance.

There is *nothing* too hard for God! I am a living witness of his grace and mercy. I no longer sleep with women, nor do I have a desire to. I see beautiful women daily, *including myself,* and they are my sisters. *They have nothing I want.* Now, a God-fearing, sold-out-for Christ type of man is definitely my desire. As they say on *Jeopardy! I'll take him for one million, Alex.*

Since I've been saved, I have come in contact with women who have tried to come on to me. I kindly let them know that sleeping with women is no longer my lifestyle, and how Jesus is a deliverer. *He pulled me out to pull out others.* I know some of you reading this are where I was, and some may be even deeper. Christ wants you to know that He can free you from this, and anything else you have going on if you give Him the chance. All you have to do is come to Him. He will clean you up.

All things are possible to those who believe.

12

The Million-Dollar Man with the Master Plan

THEY SAY EVERYTHING that glitters ain't gold, but in your case, I wasn't quite sure. You were in a lane and class all by yourself. You superseded the thoughts of many and had become just what you set out to be. You weren't the next best thing. You were the thing itself. Everywhere on the face of the earth, unless you lived under a rock, people knew your name. You broke language and cultural barriers. *Where in the world did this guy come from? Who is this man and how can I get close to him*? These were the thoughts of men and women throughout the world. Many coveted the idea of wanting to be you, or either to simply be around you. You were like a cold drink in the scorching desert. *You were refreshing*. Everyone wanted a personal encounter with you. And you knew and loved every minute of it.

All that you set your hands to do prospered. Failure was not an option. Your motto was, "Win, Win, Win and Win again." You stood out among the masses. No one had what you had, and no one could do what you did. Duplicating you wasn't even possible, even though most tried. You were the originator. You were an arrogant son of a gun, *as my grandmother would say*. But even with this flaw, people still loved you and gravitated toward your every move. Watching you was like watching a live movie. There was always nonstop movement and action. There is no doubt that you were destined to be great and to help others reach the same goal. All you had to do was stick to the blueprint. *Did you? Let's see ...*

The Day We Met

I was so scared getting out of that car knowing you were a few footsteps away, but you would have never known it. I was as cool as a cucumber. Truth be told, I could have thrown up all over you because my stomach was flip-flopping all over the place. You know how people ask if you have butterflies when you're nervous? I had butterflies, bees, and wasps! I'm surprised everyone standing next to me didn't hear my knees knocking or my heartbeat *because it sounded like the police at a drug dealer's door. I couldn't even swallow.* The lump in my throat made me feel like I had an Adam's apple. *That's how big my throat felt.* I wanted to run but I knew I had to show up. If I couldn't find the strength to do it for me, I had to do it for the girls and my family. I also knew that my manager at the time would have gone bananas if I showed any signs of being petrified. So with all of that in mind, I really didn't have a choice.

Scared and all, I had to show up and represent. *I did the thing.* I went in like it was my first and last performance. All I knew was it was game time and I was standing in front of the best, and I had to make sure I left you knowing the same. *I gave everything I had.* I wasn't leaving anything undone. I remember the few seconds I had before you walked on the elevator, and when those doors closed, I had to go for broke. Performing for you was unheard of for a girl like me, but it was now my reality and I had to give it everything I had. Realizing that this was my shot made me have to convince you that I had the talent to be great. I may not have been one of the top singers you've heard, but what I had was different and unique. I wasn't leaving without you seeing it all. I was a fifteen-year old kid who knew she had to stay the course and deliver what was deep down inside.

When those doors opened and you walked off that elevator into the lounge, it was time to go to the next level, and that next level changed my life forever. Determined to pull you into my world, my performance went through the roof. *Singing in your face, looking you in the eyes, and not backing down from your blank stares, caused you to finally smile.* I was going for broke. After the last word of the song was sung, you asked me my name and age, briefly spoke to my manager, and then thanked us for coming out. I was crushed! *Did he at least like what he heard? Dang!* Needless to say, tears, tears, tears, and more tears streamed down my face once I was alone. I thought I was a failure, but then the next morning at 5 a.m., that fateful phone call came through. *Are you serious? He called and said what?* You called the next day and said not to take us anywhere because you wanted to offer us a deal, and you kept your word. In my mind I was thinking *Lights, cameras, action. It's on and popping. I am rich!* Can someone say it with me? Wrong, wrong, wrong, and wrong again. I was awakened to the reality of work, work, work, and more work.

There were countless nights in the studio singing until my throat was dry, hoarse, and sore. I had to move away from home to become more acquainted with the girls. *This was one of the hardest things I ever had to do, but I had to put on my big girl drawers and do what was needed.* I had to attend industry parties, which weren't that bad because I got the opportunity to meet a lot of celebs, get media training, get etiquette classes, learn songs, and go to vocal training to learn how to sing from my diaphragm. *My di-a-what?* This was all new for me.

All I thought I was going to do was perform on stages, do music videos, sing and dance like Michael Jackson, and get paid out the wazoo. *You guessed it right.* My perspective on things was completely wrong. My thoughts and reality of fame were shattered. *I'm sleepy! I'm hungry! I'm tired, and I miss my family, mainly my mama. Is this what being a celebrity looks like? I didn't sign up for this. They never showed any of this stuff on TV Why do I have to do this? Can't we skip all of this and get to the good stuff?*

I can understand recording in the studio, but all of this other stuff is exhausting. Where is the stage, and where is all the money so I can buy my mama a house? I am not a fan of this nonsense—that was my name for hard work back then. *No one ever told me this was a part of being famous. All I ever saw on television was the glitz and glamour. This right here ain't glamorous at all. This is definitely not what I expected, but since I have people routing for and counting on me, I cannot let them down.*

I had to suck it up and grow up quickly, and even the more when you walked in the room. It was game time, and you made sure that no one played with your money. Time was money and money was time. When you said it was time to work, it was time to work. There were times when I wanted to be babied, but there was no time for that. You made me comfortable and nervous at the same time. I knew you didn't have time to play any games with me, so I made it a point to be on point. I was one out of a million girls who had been chosen, and if I messed it up, there were countless others who would have loved my spot, so playtime was over. You made sure I knew I had to show up and be great, while you also treated me as a big brother would treat his little sister *in your different way.* You kept me laughing with all the jokes you cracked, but you also kept me on my toes when the businessman *that you are* walked into the studio and yelled out, "Why isn't this song done?"

There were so many layers to you. You were like a box of crayons. Blue for calm, red for mad, green for peaceful, orange for rage, and black for it's about to go down. You did have your moments *when your outburst* made the entire room stand still and there would be complete silence in the air, but once it passed, it was back to work.

Those particular moments, *even though sometimes I got scared,* showed your humanity. Back then you were a superstar to me, so for me to see you angry was not normal at first. Even though I had become a part of the family, I must admit, I still had my starstruck moments. My thoughts were, Am I really connected to this man, or should I say, the man everybody loves, and/or loves to hate? You were one of the most influential men in the world, and I had been blessed with a bird's-eye view. You were incredible to watch. A true genius at his best.

You would walk in a room and change its very dynamics. I witnessed people flock to you. I saw grown men become boys around you. They would try to hold their composure and be all hardcore, but after a few words in the conversation, you would hear that little boy come out and they would be geeked about meeting you. You were the man everyone wanted to get close to, and I had been privileged with such. Not only was I privileged to know you, but I made history with you. You took me from just being Judy's baby to one of the top-known recording artists of the '90s til this day. You were the vehicle God used to help make my name great. Never in a zillion years would I have thought I could meet you face-to-face, *let alone work with you.* With all of that being said, you stuck to the blueprint that helped launch my career. Thank you for staying the course.

There is one more thing I would like to acknowledge. Now that I am older, I never thought of how heavy a load you had to carry. You not only had to live up to your own expectations, but you had to live up to the expectations of others. I can't imagine all the things you endured. I can't fathom the stress you carried just trying to live a life that exemplified greatness. As I think back on all that you were shouldering, I bless God for giving you the strength to hold up under the pressure. There were times when you showed frustration, but you always seemed to shake it off and come back fighting. *You were the hallmark card of success.* Looking at you showed others they weren't working hard enough, and every excuse given was a moment lost. Your life challenged people to go after their dreams and to make sure they were pursuing their dreams with compassion and a work ethic that said, "I won't stop until I see it come to pass." You worked around the clock, regardless of how tired you were. You were fueled with the gas of success, and everyone that stopped at your station experienced superstardom.

Your life has affected nations, and it has truly changed mine forever. Without you, people throughout the world would not know me, and for that I am forever grateful to God for using you. I will always love and respect you, no matter how mad I've been with you at times. I was mad because of how easy it was for you to drop the love *I thought* you had for me. It hurt big time to know that the brother I thought I had wasn't a brother at all but a poser. To say the least, I've been mistreated in a lot of ways by you, and it still has the capacity to hurt sometimes *if I dwell on it*, but I don't.

> I've forgiven you. I can't and won't allow who you are to cause me to become someone different, due to your unjust ways. I just have to remain consistent with being the new person I am in Christ and trust God to deal with you justly. I'm praying for you because I wanna see you become the man you say you are, but your heart is far from it. Please know that me speaking my truths doesn't negate how I feel about you. I love you and I always will. I'm just finally going to be real with myself and call you what I've seen and known for years. Even with knowing something was wrong, I stood by you. Standing by you in all the tough times, I now see meant nothing, well, at least on your behalf. No kudos to me. I was just doing what family does.
>
> I'll never forget the day your righthand man with the bald head laughed at me and told me I sound like (one of my label mates who also had gotten saved). He said this because after the group and I disbanded, I came to you for a solo deal. I was so confident in God that I was able to be a solo artist who could make you lots of money that I came to you first and was like, "We can do this," but you never even thought to meet with me. It was as if we never had a

> relationship. If I wasn't singing and dancing to your tune, the song was over. I'm not mad for you not signing me. What hurt is that after all the years and all the money you earned from my contribution in your life, you wouldn't even give me five minutes of your time to converse about my future goals. And how I found out things was a no-go was another slap in the face. I called back your man a week or so later asking if he spoke to you. And his reply, and I quote, was, "He said he don't wanna do it." That crushed me. I knew then that I meant nothing to you.
>
> Ten-plus years later we saw each other, and you came at me with that same smile spewing out words about us always being family. And there I was again, right back in your mental grip believing every word, which left me high and dry once you got what you wanted and the shows were over. I'm not the only one you spoke these lying words to. So many of us can attest to your empty words.

Even with all of that being said, I've learned some valuable nuggets from you. You've taught me no matter what the odds are against me, or what it looks or feels like, stay the course. If people leave, stay the course, if I have to do it alone, stay the course, if I fall down *get up* and stay the course, because it'll all pan out in the end. I can't stop and I won't stop is just two prolific statements I've learned from a man who has the potential to be such a great teacher, *if you weren't so selfish.*

I've also learned this beautiful gem from you as well. When doing business, I must always remain in a business posture no matter who the person is. I learned this particular nugget the hard way, yet I've learned it. You told me we were family and I believed you, which made me trust everything you said. But little did I know, I was the only one believing that family existed between you and me. By trusting you I left myself wide open with my guard down for you to plunder me in areas of business I knew nothing about. But one thing I won't do is blame you for everything. I should have done my part in business, and because I didn't uphold such, I got robbed of a lot. Experience has the potential to be a great teacher and you have taught me well. With that being said, thank you for all that I've learned.

My concluding thoughts: What was once a little boy's dream. You took courage and mixed it with perseverance and became a mogul. That, my friend is a *phenom.* But somewhere along the line you got tainted and instead of you helping others reach their dream, you begin to steal them. Not sure what happened to you, but I hope you get back your heart of innocence.

#Love

13

The Day I Said Yes

IT ALL HAPPENED SO QUICKLY. Well not really. There I was living my life like it was golden, doing whatever I wanted, whenever I wanted to do it. *The world was mine, so to speak.* I had everything I thought I could have wanted, even people at my very fingertips. I was living what I thought was the American dream. I was traveling the world, singing on stages throughout the land, and was now a household name globally. Everywhere I went I heard people screaming my name. *This is the life*, so I thought. You couldn't tell me I wasn't the best thing since cooked food walking on earth. The arrogance that hid behind my false humility was ugly but very hard to spot if you weren't in tune with God. I was feeling myself. I thought life was all about me, *but I was about to find out how wrong I was.*

I had everything I wanted and more. *I had become greedy for gain.* Even with all I had, I still had this sense of unfulfillment, so I went harder to obtain what I thought I was missing. I began to have more drinks, more sex, brought more clothes, and I even gained more so-called "friends." *Now that should have been sufficient, but to my surprise I was still empty. These things didn't have any real depth, but I guess it'll do for now.* Masking my true feelings was something I had become a pro at for years, so I'll just continue to hide my feelings. *This was a piece of cake to do.*

To the average person on the outside looking in, I had it all. What could a girl with my status need? Little did people know how I was falling apart at the seams. Underneath the facade of me loving my life, I was slowly dying. I was so unhappy with who and what I had become, but I didn't know how to express it, nor get out of it. I tried to ignore and silence my pain by being inebriated when I was alone, but it always wore off. During my quiet time is when I had to deal with my demons and personally at the time, I didn't want or know how to face myself. *So, I'd drink.* I would drink so I wouldn't have to think about my reality. These were some of the worse moments for me, but when I got past them, I was right back to my old ways.

A few things along the way started pricking at my heart and made me begin to question if I was a bad person. These thoughts were something new because I never considered myself bad. I did good things for people, and I felt like I was good because I wasn't killing, stealing, or hurting people physically (with the exception of fighting those I was in a relationship with at the time). Overall, I was a good-hearted person who didn't go out looking for trouble. I believe I am a peaceable person.

My first eye-opening moment came when a young lady I was dating called me evil. She and I were at home, and, of course, I had been drinking. We got into it. This was one of those nights I'd had a lot to drink and I was going off. I jumped in her face and I began to act way out of character. I don't know what she saw in me, but she began to back up and back away from me with this look of terror on her face. She repeated these words to me over and over again, "Don't touch me! Oh my God, *you are so evil!*" When she said it the first time, it made me jump in her face even more. I was smoking upset, but when she began to ball herself up in a corner and act like she was extremely afraid of me, I was startled. I was still yelling in her face, but in my head I was like, *Why is she saying this to me? I'm not an evil person, I love God.* Because of her response, I backed off, and when I was out of her presence, it played on my mind. I had never been called anything of the sort, and this was something that hit me like a ton of bricks. However, a few days later, I was back to my regular routine.

As I continued down this road of self-destruction and believing that the world was mine, there was one last voice I believed helped put the icing on the cake to cause me to take a look in the mirror—the voice of my mom. My mom wasn't the type of person to call you out, she was more private and would tell me she needed to speak to me. Every time I heard her say those words, I wanted to disappear. I didn't want to face her because I knew she was going to speak the truth, and she would also be able to see through every lie I told. I'll never forget her words this one particular time we spoke. She began to tell me how she was disappointed in what I was becoming and how she didn't raise me to be like this. She began to tell me I knew better and so on and so forth, but the words that stung and cut through me is when my best friend, *my mama*, told me that she loved me but didn't like me. All I could do was sit there and allow the tears to stream down my face. She was hurt and so was I. I couldn't believe I had hurt the very one I was trying so hard to please.

I remember her telling me how material possessions meant nothing to her. *She didn't care if I had millions of dollars.* She loved me, not what I had accomplished. As our conversation came to an end, I hugged her and of course she loved on me, but once I was out of her sight I cried like a baby. My feelings were crushed. Her words never left my psyche.

I wish I could tell you that right after this conversation with my mama I was back on the right track, but I wasn't. I actually got worse. Instead of me being off the hook, I was now off the chain! I was down and ready for whatever. Months went by, actually a few more years and then one day, someone walked into my life and interrupted everything.

The second album had just been released and the single was doing great. I was on my way to a ridiculous level of fame. It was the next level that I had been waiting on. Everyone was super hyped about where they saw this album going. Everything on the outside was looking great. We had the greatest forecast concerning the album, yet I still had this issue of emptiness. *Why am I feeling like this?* I began to ask questions about me being a nice person and realized how I needed to change some things in my life. I started feeling really different and very emotional about God. I recall talking to my brother and telling him that I needed to change. At this time in my life I remember feeling tired every day I woke up. Every time someone asked me how I was doing my reply would be, "Tired." Some way or another those words would find their way to my lips. Day in and day out, this had become my story. But one morning I woke up and I was never the same again.

I was standing in the mirror looking at myself. It was me, but it wasn't me. I could see that it was clearly my image but something about me was so unrecognizable. I stood there trying to figure out what was wrong. I don't know why, but I had this heaviness on me, and I began to cry. *I cried the whole day.* I went back to my brother and told him these words, "I can't do this anymore, I'm about to give my life to God." His reply was, "Okay baby." I left his presence in tears. I didn't know what to do but the tears wouldn't stop. I knew something needed to be done, but I didn't know what. I remember hearing these words in my spirit, "If you don't give me your life, you're going to die." *It was faint like a whisper.*

I began to cry harder but that's when I said yes. *The yes that I gave was to God.* I didn't literally open my mouth and say yes, but my heart said yes. I was crying so hard that I couldn't say yes verbally, but my heart truly cried out to Him to help me. I was done with doing things my way and I needed Him. In that very moment I knew something happened because I felt different.

I went on with the rest of my day, but when I woke up the next morning, I was totally different. It was as if someone turned the lights on. So many of the old things I had a love for had left me. My urge to drink was gone, my potty mouth was gone, and my desire to get to know God was stronger than ever. What just happened to me? Can someone please let me know? I had opened up my heart to Jesus and when I said "Yes," he saved me. From that very moment, my life has never been the same. I've been walking with Jesus ever since.

Giving my life to Christ was the best decision I've ever made in my life. By the grace of God, I've had great accomplishments that God has blessed me with. Being signed by Diddy, and being a member of the R&B group Total, just to name a few. I'm nothing short of thankful, but *nothing* can ever top the day I made the decision to invite this amazing Man into my life. I can't even begin to explain how I felt. It seemed as if someone came and lifted weights off of my entire being.

Even the complexion of my skin went from having this dark overcast, to a glow that could not be dimmed. *Something happened to me that I cannot even try to explain.* I encountered something, or should I say someone who changed me the moment I said "Yes." And that someone is Jesus Christ the Son of God.

I won't lie and say there hasn't been days that I get frustrated and I may sometimes feel like quitting. But when I have these days, the Holy Spirit rises up within me and begins to encourage me to keep going forward. I have this burning on the inside that says I can do all things with Christ. *Nothing is impossible with Him, so it makes me press even harder.*

I've come to the understanding that life is not easy.

We will all experience the good, the bad, and the ugly. If you have yet to experience the bad and the ugly, *keep on living, as my great grandmother would say.* Those days will show up and when they do, if you have Jesus in your life. He will turn your pain into victory, and your tears into a shout of praise to God. You can always be sure of this one thing. "You will always have the victory when you roll with him, because he has overcome the world."

There will come a time when we all will need someone strong enough to bear the burden of what we are facing, and I *repeat* and *scream* to you that his name is Jesus! He is able to carry the weight of the world on His shoulders. He came into the world to do so.

Please hear me when I say this, one day we will all stand before God and give an account of our lives. And upon that account will determine our outcome. *Heaven or hell, it's our choice. All he's looking for is a yes not perfection.*

I know that it's not protocol, but right now I need to ask you this question. If you died right now, *and some people around the world, sad to say, just did,* where would you go? Most people would say heaven. Others would dare to say that they're going to a better place. Let me leave you with this. I heard a man say, "Good people go to hell and only saved people go to heaven." We can believe that we are good all day long, but by who's standard, God's or ours? There is a way to God and that way is singular. There are not multiple ways to get to him and the way is through his perfect and precious gift, *his Son Jesus Christ,* and all are invited. All you have to do is say, "Yes." God is waiting to change your life just like he did mine and millions of others. He loves you and desires a relationship with you.

Don't let this moment pass you by because who knows if you'll ever get another?

#WillyouSayYes

14

Finding P-Girl

WHO AM I? *What a question to ask yourself when you think that you're solid on the answer.* What if there was a chance that you've been living a lie and the confidence you have in knowing yourself could be at risk of dwindling away? *How would you feel?* Well, that's exactly what happened to me.

Rude Awakening

Hold on a minute! What do you mean? *This is an inward conversation that I'm having with God as He starts to download and reveal my truths to me.* You mean to tell me that everything I was judged on, ridiculed about, and even praised for, is not who I am?

What about all those hours I put in at the gym beating up on my body? Or how about all the hours I sat in the chair at the salon getting my hair done making sure that every piece of hair was in place?

And let's not forget about the thousands of dollars spent on clothes so that I was dressed to impress? If this is not who I am, then who am I? Since you're saying that I'm not my face, my skin tone, my clothes, shoes, body or hair, then why have I been defined as such almost all of my life? I honestly thought this defined me. That's why I worked so hard at it. And now in the prime of my life, you tell me that this is not who I am? *Are you serious?*

Millions of questions swarm my mind like bees, and I need answers. I feel as if someone has pulled the rug from underneath me and snatched away my identity, and now I stand here left alone to pick up all the scattered pieces. My perfect puzzle has been dismantled and my vulnerability is in the air.

Could this be the answer to the prayer I prayed when I asked God to unclog my heart and show me the real me? *I was not presuming this to be the outcome, but I can't ignore what's being revealed.* This doesn't feel good at all. I feel naked and exposed. I want to put on my sneakers and run as far away as I can, but I know that that won't solve anything. On one hand I'm very thankful to God for exposing me because due to the exposure I can finally deal with my truths, and on the other hand I am embarrassed, hurt, and upset because of the state of my reality. I have so many mixed emotions right now. I'm not sure if I should laugh, cry, scream, or shout for joy based upon my new discovery.

I've heard people talk about the joy of discovery and how beautiful it is to find out the unknown, but there is also another side to it. *Discovery won't always leave a smile on your face; it can actually cause you to wish that you never found out what has been disclosed.* Truth be told, I'm still in awe of how I've been deceived all of these years and what gets me the most is that I'm the culprit. It feels like I got punched in the face about hundred times by a fist named truth. I never saw it coming because in my mind, I had it all together. For all these years I never knew I was playing dress up. *Dress up was a game I played when I was a little girl.* I would put on some of my mom's clothes and a pair of her shoes, and I would act like I was an adult. In that moment no one could tell me anything different, I was grown. I can relate this to my current identity. I dressed up my outer man for so long that that's who I became, not knowing that it was a false identity. *But when it wasn't dressed to the T, I was disheveled and lost.*

This is crushing me because I truly thought I knew who I was. I can't turn back now because I want to know the truth. And not just to know it but take the next step to getting free from the bondages of deception. Even though this is not the most favorable discovery there is a peace rising up on the inside that is causing the turbulence to subside. I believe that the only reason why I'm experiencing peace is because I stand in agreement with what has been revealed.

> If I am to be completely honest, when I sat still and pondered on things, I do understand why I'm being hit with these thunderous blows. It's time for me to man up concerning the truth about myself, if I desire to be free. There are two outcomes that can come from this. Either I can be grateful that I'm being confronted so that change can occur, or I'm going to be proud and haughty and continue to lie to myself and bury the truth.
>
> The only issue I have with dealing with past hurts is that once you start digging, much more than what you've expected tends to rise to the surface. However, I can't allow that to be my focus. The result of dealing with my issues is freedom and that's what I want. The process may not be the easiest, but the benefits will outweigh the cost. I don't know about you but I'm ready to see the real me. Just think about it this way, if I've gotten this far based upon me not knowing the real me, how much further am I about to go knowing who I really am?

With the Lord causing me to go deeper, I finally understand why I had such an obsession with perfection. Everything I did had to be perfect. If it wasn't perfect, according to my standards, then it wasn't of value. *Ain't that something*? Someone who was so broken and so sensitive has the nerve to be shallow. *What an awkward combination.* I tried so hard to divert from showing pain, that every once in a while, the truth would seep through. The real reason why I always strived for perfection was because I always felt inadequate. I never thought I was good enough.

Everything for me always seemed to come so hard. I was the one in school who had to go to speech therapy. When it came to homework my sister had to help me, which I hated. For me to really grasp things I had to sometimes hear it over and over again so that I could comprehend, and when it came to the matters of the heart. I was always the last to be found by love. The misconceptions I had about myself, made me angry and competitive. I had to be the best, so I worked my butt off in everything I did. What I didn't know was that because of me dealing with my brokenness in the wrong way it was stealing my true identity.

Now don't get me wrong, I am well known for having the poppin' hairstyles, the clothes, and the body, but there is more to me than what one sees. Because of me having such a negative outlook it caused my outcome to be the same, and it didn't stop there. I began to judge people for their hang-ups. *It wasn't something that I did every day, but I did do my fair share of indulging.* I had my opinions on what they should be doing and how they needed to get it done. My way was the best way to ensure the best outcome. *If this ain't the pot calling the kettle black, then I don't know what is! This is wrong on every level.* You would think because I knew what it felt like to be an outcast, that I would have compassion for others, but that was far from the case. I was the one waiting to crack my whip on the most fragile person. Why would I make someone else feel the way I felt? I remember so clearly that feeling of worthlessness. Why would I do something like this, especially knowing how it feels? What I now know and understand is that hurt people hurt people. I was doing to others what I felt was being done to me.

I remember making fun of people who were overweight. Joking and talking about those my homies and I said were ugly. I made sure to be front and center, and even sometimes the ringleader of the jokes. The very words that I cried over were the words I used to victimize others. I can think back on the times I laughed at the girls who had what we called, nappy hair. I would go all the way in with the disrespect which I then called "humorous fun." I laughed at those whose parents couldn't afford name brand clothes or shoes. Whatever took me out of a negative spotlight was fine with me as long as I wasn't the recipient, I was down for the get down. I had become the very person I despised. I had moments of feeling bad, but I didn't have the confidence to be a leader, so I followed. All I knew was that I was now a part of the who's who, and I wasn't going to go against the grain.

Doing the Right Thing

I want to openly apologize too those that I've scarred. I would have never indulged in such behavior had I just recalled that I was once you and that you were me. Life can be so funny at times because it makes no logical sense how a person who felt the pain of rejection and loneliness would turn around and express the same life-altering criticisms to others. A cycle will repeat itself if there is no one present to change its course.

I can transparently conclude that my mind is still being renewed in this area one day at a time. Every time I inwardly hear the words, *you're inadequate,* I must remind myself that the devil is a liar and speak the opposite. Some days are better than others, but I'm determined to know the truth. I will no longer lie down and wait for things to change; I have a part to play in obtaining and maintaining my victory.

Repeat This Prayer

Father God, in the precious name of Jesus, I ask that you hear my heart. I've thought these destructive thoughts for many years, and they have become my truth. I've felt this way for a good bit of my life, but

I do believe that you're able to help me. I'm asking you to heal me in every area of my spirit, heart, mind, body, and soul. I've carried this weight for way too long and I'm finally ready to let it go. I no longer believe the lies that I was told and the lies that the devil does not want me to let go of. You are my Creator and because you say that I am adequate then that's what I am. I let go of every lie I've embraced as my truth. Today is the day that I say, "No more!" No more accepting or embracing anything that is contrary to what you say. I'm ready to fight for my freedom in every area of my life, especially in this area because it's held me down and suffocated me for years. I love you and I praise you for loving me enough to pull me out. I glorify and honor you for who you are. I know that some days will be harder than others but it's worth fighting for, and you also said in your word, *the Bible*, that you would never leave me nor forsake me. I trust you Lord to do just what you said. If it wasn't for you, I don't know what or whom I'd be right now. I could have been the one in the mental institution who lost her mind, or the prostitute on the street corner, dead or in jail, but you intervened on my behalf when I wasn't even thinking of you. Thank you, Father, for keeping me. Please don't ever let me go. Please don't allow me to live life without you. I give you permission to turn my world upside down and inside out so that I may be erected into what you have called me to be for your glory. I yield and surrender to your rebuilding process. I seal this prayer in the Mighty name Jesus Christ, Son of the Living God!

Amen

15

Big Fish

IF ONLY YOU KNEW what you were to me, you would have never left. You would have realized that everything you ever wanted was on the inside of me. I would have done my hardest to provide you with anything. You truly didn't understand that you had a woman so beaten down by life that she would have done anything to please you, even if it meant giving you everything.

Since you had become one of the closest people to me, I valued you above myself. I would tell myself that you gave me significance and because that was my mindset, you could have had it all. But because you viewed me as worthless, you left.

Back then I thought it was one of the worst things that could have happened to me, but today I bless God for breaking my heart and allowing you to leave. I've come to understand that had you stayed, I would've never found me. *Today I love myself more than I ever have, and my stock keeps going up.* My love for self is making me rich beyond material goods. I am rich with self-worth, and God knows this was an area of my life that I was piss pot poor in. I never thought I would be able to say this to you and truly mean it from my heart, *but I say it today with all sincerity*: Thank you for leaving me! It forced me to step up to the plate and see myself. This was necessary for me to become a better woman. I could never thank you enough for the strength you do not know and won't ever understand that you gave me by disrespecting, degrading, and cheating on me. It forced me to dig deep and ask myself why I put up with all the crap you threw.

Upon doing some soul-searching, my ugly truth surfaced. I recognized that I put up with your mess because I felt privileged to be with someone who looked like you. It wasn't about your social status because I wasn't a gold digger. It did have a good bit to do with you being a handsome man who wanted what I thought was the ugly girl. I knew I wasn't the type of female you were used to dating. I knew because you made sure you told me that I wasn't the type you would usually choose, but it was just something about me. Then you would end it by saying that I was the prettiest woman in the world. *Whatever. Was I supposed to believe that*? You had no idea the harm your words did to me, but I kept my mouth closed and never mentioned to you how it damaged my thoughts of myself even the more. You made me feel ugly, stupid, dumb, and unvalued all at the same time. I was so lost with you, but I honestly would have stayed had you not kicked me to the curb. How is it that I was willing to stay in a place that was sucking the vitality from me? That sounds so harsh but it's the truth. You threw me away like I was a bag of trash.

Maybe it was something you did intentionally. Maybe you knew exactly what you were doing. Or just maybe your plan was to break me and continue to make me weaker than I already was so you could rule over me. Yeah, that's it, because you told your boy that that was your plan. *You told him I was too close to my mom and you were going to break me.* If you don't recall that conversation, just think on the people we both know. He sold you out when you finally betrayed him. *It's so much that I found out after the fact, but that's old news.* You are who you are. Anyhoo...

I remember the day that we met, or should I say the day I replied. *Who is this dude contacting me on social media telling me, "Thus saith the Lord?" I don't know who you are, nor do I know what you want, so I'll pass.* At least that's what my mouth said at first. A few weeks went by and there you were again with another message. For whatever reason, and I don't know why, this time it sparked my interest enough to at least find out who you were. I googled you to see if you were who you said you were, and come to find out, you were telling me the truth. Once I had confirmation, I finally hit you back to see what you wanted. You told me, in a few words, that if there was anything you could do to help me, you were willing. To say the least, this really touched me. In the industry I'm in, people throw you away quick when they think you're no longer relevant. I don't recall how we ended up having a phone conversation, but after having one, you seemed pretty cool. In the midst of us talking, you asked me about doing music together, so we played around with a few dates to see when we could meet up—*after prayer, because I didn't know if you were crazy, and after a conversation with my family, so they would know my whereabouts.* After us talking over the particulars for the trip, we set a date.

I'm now sitting on a plane with feelings of anxiousness due to me being a little nervous about meeting up with you. Let me calm down because I know that I made the right decision to come, I'm just having a moment of the jitters. I deplane and walk to baggage claim to retrieve my luggage and then I think to myself, *I have no idea who is picking me up!* I call your cell phone and you tell me you are pulling around. As I'm standing on the curb waiting, I look up and see a man hanging out of a car window. The closer it gets, I realize that it's you.

You were beautiful. I know that men are supposed to be called handsome *and you were*, but my description of you when I first saw you was beauty. You greeted me with so much love that I felt like I knew you. I expected you to be arrogant and full of yourself, but you were quite the opposite. You had this sincerity about you that pulled on me when you hugged me. It was a little eerie for me at first. I felt something for you the moment you hugged me, and since that has never happened before, it stumped me. I quickly gathered myself and continued as if everything was cool. I jumped in the car so that we could get to where we needed to be, and the whole car ride we talked and laughed about everything. *Have we met before? Do I know you?* That's how comfortable I felt being around you.

As we continued to flow, I looked in your eyes and had a moment. I began to wonder if you could feel what I felt when you hugged me and if so, what were your thoughts on it. *Come on, Pamela... Get yourself together!* I had to talk to myself because I didn't want to overthink anything. And I did not want to use any flattering words to try and win him over or get him to like me. I inwardly encouraged myself to be easy. By the time I finished having my side bar conversation, we had finally arrived at the destination. After a long day in the studio, you drove me to my hotel room. We sat and spoke briefly in the lobby about the possibilities that could come from us working together, and once the conversation ended, I went upstairs and you went home.

When I opened the door to my room, I was not expecting what I saw. There were some gifts left for me on the bed. I sat down so I could open them up, and what I found inside had me in utter shock. I opened up a pink box and found a beautiful letter and book inside, *which made my heart melt.* Your letter was so sweet and thoughtful. The way you talked about me really moved me. It meant so much because you took the time to go out of your way and type a letter for me. And you also purchased a book with the theme of staying close to God. I was in awe!

> Writing letters and giving gifts must be your thing. I see that I'm not the only one who has experienced this. It seems to be pattern of yours.

But what came next literally had me stuck. As I reread the letter and sat there silent, I saw this grayish-looking plastic envelop that was still in the box. When I opened it up, a thousand dollars fell out. *No way! You've got to be kidding me!* You had no idea that I was financially going through a tough time and was in need of a blessing, but God knew. All I could do was give God praise and thank him for meeting my need. There was also something you told me to do with the money that had me shaking my head. *This man is amazing*. You told me to take ten percent of it and give it to whomever God led me to, and the rest was for me. Those words took me overboard. I couldn't believe that you were looking for the blessing you gave me to keep on blessing others. God knows that this is truly my heart, so at this point I was in total bliss. I immediately picked up my phone and called my mom and began to share with her what you did. *The tears dropped down my face*. I couldn't believe what had just happened. It was all so unexpected. Once I gathered myself, I hung up with my mom and called you. I thanked you for everything, and of course the waterworks came down again. Your response to me was, "To God be all the glory."

I flew back home the next day not knowing if I would see you again and if so, when. You were really a nice guy and I would have wanted for us to get to know more about each other, but I wasn't going to say anything and look desperate. I got back home in one piece and shared with my family that meeting you was great. I called to let you know that I was safe and that's when you told me you were going to be off of the radar for a while because there were some things you needed to pray about. *No problem at all, I'll talk to you soon*. During the time of us not speaking, I started noticing something about me that I hadn't done concerning any other dude. I was talking about you morning, noon, and night. I didn't even realize it until my mom brought it to my attention. That's when I knew I was really feeling you. I went about my business trying not to think about you, and next thing I know, I get a phone call. When I saw your number on my phone I was as happy as a pig rolling around in slop, *as my mom would say.* But ya' girl had to play it cool. You called to see if I would be willing to fly back out but this time for about four to five days. You explained to me everything that you were going to set up so that we could make the best of the trip and get as much work done as possible. Needless to say, I flew out a couple weeks later and the trip was a success.

While I was there working something very unusual took place, you professed your love for me. *What did this man just say to me?* I am trying my best not to cry but the tears flooded my eyes. My thoughts are hurdling my brain. They were leaping all over the place. I didn't know what to say to you. This was some fairytale movie type stuff. Has my prince arrived? You took my hand and continued to speak your heart as I sat there in tears. You reassured me that you knew I was the one for you without any doubts, and I should take time to pray and find out the same. *What? I'm in shock.* That's when you lifted up your sleeve and showed me the tattoo you got on your arm that had my name on it. You explained how you were up for three days straight at your house and God told you I was your wife. But I also have this memory of the tattoo. I clearly recall the day you got it covered with black ink for me not doing what you said.

It was really difficult for me to believe that you were into me the way that you were because of my own insecurities. Why would someone like you be interested in me, especially with this skin condition that I'm visibly going through right now? *That's another story altogether.* I thought to myself, *I guess I'll go along for the ride, or until he decides to stop playing games.* But to my surprise, you stayed consistent. Every time you spoke to me, it was with tenderness and care. It was almost as if you studied me and learned how to speak my language of love. Your words were like music being sung into my ears. You knew the exact tone and pitch to use when you addressed me, and that alone had my full attention. The more we talked, the more I was pulled in and intrigued by you. Your press to get close to me was exciting. You made it a point that I knew you were serious about wanting to be with me.

There was no cost to your pursuit of me. You traveled back and forth to see me like I was the girl next door. So many hours were spent back and forth on planes to prove your love. *Yes! This was all I ever wanted. Someone finally sees my worth and wants me for me and not for what I have or who I am.* Just the thought of that made my face light up. I had an inward smile that could not be tamed or taken away. I had no desire for anyone else. I had to prepare for what I felt. Hopefully I wasn't tripping. I guess I'll soon find out.

I tried my hardest to hide that I was either falling for or infatuated with you. I was secretly anticipating what was to come but I had to stay calm and not get ahead of myself. You seemed to be everything I prayed for, but I still was a little unsure.

Your outer shell was perfect. You were unique. Everything about you, I thought, was heaven sent. You were stunning! You showcased excellence. What a prize. You weren't some regular ole fish from the sea. You had to have come from special waters. Wherever you swam from, I'm glad to make your acquaintance. To sum it up,

#YouWereBreathtaking

You were the most polite, tender, and gentle catch that has ever dealt with me. Your care for me was nurturing and delicate. It was soothing to my soul. You had me sold. You had me quoting lines from the movie *Color Purple* like: "Harpo, who this man?" I was adorned by your attention, love, and care. *All a girl wants. I've finally come face-to-face with my knight in shining armor.* You were so into me that I sometimes waited for the rug to be swept from under me because this was just surreal. *Does this Big Fish really love me?* The consistency of your interest in me was seasoned with class and grace. Your conversation was dope. You took charge without making me feel less than. You were a man's man. Everything I thought I was unworthy of having was now in my grasp. My heart was sealed.

My protector! My friend! My love! Let's journey out babe. And journey we did. I didn't know who you were at the time nor did I know your arrival date, but when you finally manifested, I knew that it was you. The commonality that we shared was mind blowing. We shared the same views, thoughts, same favorite color, foods, and most importantly our faith in God.

I was trying my best to slow down my thoughts of us being one, but the more I tried, the more they excelled. Could you be the one I asked for? Or were you trying to get close to me because I'm Pam from Total? There were times when I didn't express how I felt about you because I didn't want to look foolish. I also had a few reservations that shied me away from telling you how I felt, due to the games I encountered in old relationships. I thought you were going to be the same way. My doubts were, *Is he trying to sleep with me? Is he trying to get me to open up to him and then walk away? Is it because my name holds more weight in the industry than his? Or is he really genuine?*

Because of me having these adverse thoughts, I made sure that my walls were up, but every time I talked to you, they came down a little more. I tried my best to keep them up, but you kept breaking through. Your laugh, your smile, and your sweet words made me want to trust you. I don't know what it was about you, but I couldn't keep you at a distance. Maybe it was because I had seen my lion's share of rotten fish and your freshness made me gravitate to you. You stood up for me and that was something I never had from a man. Mostly, all they ever did was take from me and you came to the table giving and not looking for anything in return. At least not in those sacred moments.

I felt your heart and it scared me, but it also made me question God and ask him if you were the one. I was excited and ready to see what was next. Was it just "gas," as the old folks would say, or was it a divine connect? Was I falling in love with the thought of being in love or was I falling in love with you? I told myself I wasn't going to fall hard and that I was going to take my time, but I didn't even try to control what was going on. Being with you for those short months seemed like we were together forever, and what came next only happens in the movies.

It all took place the day I came back into the country from Dominican Republic with my homegirl. Just to give ya'll a little brief summary of my trip, it was great except, for my run in with something that caused my face to flare up and cause me to look like I was deformed. Remember that skin condition I mentioned earlier in this chapter? Well it flared up and caused my face to swell one size bigger than what it was. I had open sores all over it that were leaking puss. My eyes were almost closed shut, my face was literally raw, *pink flesh was showing*, and I had to get on a plane to come back to the States. I spoke to you on the phone and told you all of what was going on and sent you a picture and your words were, "I know who you are. This will all clear up." To my surprise, you told me you were coming to my hometown to take care of me. I begin to cry because I didn't want you to see me this way. You told me on the phone that everything was going to be okay, but I was dreading you seeing me like this. I cried even more when you said you wanted to take care of me.

I finally get back to the States and guess who says he is picking me up from the airport? You! Omg! You call my phone and let me know that you are waiting for me outside of baggage claim. I gather my things and call to let you know I'm coming out. As I'm walking, I'm scared out of my wits because I know once you see me, you're out. *People throughout the airport are staring at me because I am a sight to see.* I never, ever felt like such an outcast. I look up and there you are. You walk up to me in the middle of the crowd, kiss me, take my bags, and hug me back to the car. *Wait a minute, wait a minute, wait just a doggone minute! Don't you see what I look like?*

You didn't even acknowledge what I have going on. We drive off and head toward our destination. We stop by my mom's job and she comes out to greet me, and her face says it all. Her embrace brings me to tears. Without her saying anything, I know her heart is saying, "What the heck happened to my baby?!" For you not to say a word was out of this world.

The day went on. We settled in at the hotel. We turned on the television and I remember sitting on the bed. I believe I ordered us some food and then you called me over to the couch so that we could talk. I did not want to look you in your face because of how I was looking, and your words were something like, "Girl, please, come here." You hugged and kissed on me and began to talk.

While sitting on the couch, you continued to profess your love for me. You then went inside of your pocket and pulled out a Zale's jewelry box and repeated the words of your son that you sent me in a video form a few days prior. It was a video of him saying, "Pam, will you marry my daddy please?" It absolutely melted my heart, and now his daddy was asking me the very same words. *Are you serious? Of course I will. Yes, yes, yes!*

This was imprinted in my mind as one of the highlights of my life. It was awesome to behold. And it was also sexy to behold. That night I looked at you and I couldn't wait to be your Mrs, if all went well. I was in heaven. I had mentally checked out for a minute. *My dream man is sitting right next to me and he is mine and I am his.* I had to pull my thoughts together because I was ready to give you all of me that night, but I knew I had to maintain my integrity in Christ. *Help me, Lord Jesus*! Sexing you was a no-no, because I truly stand by no sex before marriage. And I'm not talking about being engaged to be able to indulge, but after the marriage vows are complete and the pastor says, "I now pronounce you husband and wife." Then them clothes can hit the floor every day when necessary. *Yes God*!

It's something how the naked eye is unable to see beyond the surface. All I saw was the beauty of who you were. I believed that it was your total makeup. Boy, oh boy, was I in for a treat. I would have never thought that such a great catch could have so many internal issues. The unforeseen stench was about to rear its ugly head, and I was totally unaware of what was to come. I never thought the prize I was so in awe of could have the potential of becoming distorted in my sight.

Now that we were one, things began to change and change fast. At first it was a little something here and there, but then came the head spinning "who is this" type of change. Arguments emerged, tempers flared, and disagreements became the norm. The fight to change me into someone I was not was on and popping. *Who is this person? I've never met this person until now. I did not sign up for this.*

The on-again and off-again love had become a daily ritual. The beautiful love language you spoke over me in the beginning had now drastically turned. You affectionately took my name Pamela, and sweetly nicknamed me Mela. But within a matter of months, I went from Mela to being someone you now seemed to despise. Your term of endearment had turned into cuss words. *How has this become your language of love? Not one time while you were swimming in the water to catch me did I ever hear you use such language, but now that you have me, it's your frequent lingo.* You spoke without any sorrow, especially when you got mad. You were mean and vicious.

You were well versed in hiding your true identity. You appeared in the form of a harmless goldfish, but it didn't take long to find out that you were a killer-shark who was waiting for the right moment to go in for the kill. There I was swimming in my own little pond and from out of the blue you showed up to swim with me. The Big Fish has chosen me. Out of all the fish in the sea you wanted me. But now that you had me, you wanted to dominant me and because you realized you couldn't make me yield.

You wanted out.

What happened to you? This is the question I asked myself over and over again for months. What a vast extreme! What in the world could have caused such a drastic change? Was it change or was this really you? My Mamma use to say, "Whatever is in the dark, will always come to light." *She ain't never lied.*

There were others in your life that could have warned me of your colors, but they chose, and still choose to remain silent. I actually think this was their way of escaping the torment of your wrath. *Just let Pam deal with him now.* The reason why you got so mad with me and I got hit with such hurtful words was because I wasn't a part of your yes-man team. I didn't agree with your wrong treatment of others, and I wasn't going to let you rule my life. I finally get it. I now understand that you were just spoiled and acted out like a kid when he can't have his way.

I am not saying that I was completely innocent in the marriage because that would be a lie, but I wasn't vicious. That's not who I am, nor who I ever was to you. *There were times that I should have closed my mouth and trusted God, but I didn't.* I had my ways about me that were controlling and stubborn as well, but I never made you feel like an outcast. So many times, I felt like I was nothing but a whore with a hole that you would dump into. You were very aware of this statement because I said it to you quite often. *I no longer belonged to me. I belonged to you and you made sure I knew it.* I was a modern-day Tina and you were my Ike. I no longer felt loved. I felt nasty and used.

You know exactly how you treated me. Although you will deny it, me, you, and God know the truth. I truly hope you have repented from what you've done to me because I didn't deserve for you to misuse me the way you did at times. It took years to remove the stains you left on my soul. There really is a God and he loved me back to life after you nearly took it from me. You had me believing that I was a worthless piece of @$%&#. I don't and can't place all the blame on you, because I never should have married you. I never should have said yes. That's not a dig at you, it's just facts. I jumped into something I knew nothing about, and I connected myself to a man I didn't know.

Please know that I forgive you. I hold nothing in my heart against you. Little do you know you have taught me a lot. I've learned how to become a stronger woman who loves and appreciates herself and it's all because of you. The devil had a plan to destroy me by using you, but it didn't work. He wanted me to become docile and stripped of the strength I have from God, but his plan didn't work! God had me covered, even when I wanted to die. *No weapon formed against me shall prosper.* I finally understand that you only treated me badly because of all the hurt, lies, denial, insecurities, and demons that reside on the inside of you. I am praying for you. I desire to see you set free and delivered from those demons you house.

The man that I met in the beginning is a good one, and I hope you stop trying to put on a show for everyone else and let him shine forth. Upon you doing so, many people will be happy with who you are and so will you.

There was a time when I didn't want to live without you, and now I bless God that I don't have to live with you. You almost broke me, but God blocked it! Your story is that you left me, but God told me, He pulled me out! I am so grateful for such a loving Father who knows what's best for his daughter. I'm praying for you, *I really am* because I realize you have been stuck in this way of life for a long time, and it's really all you've ever known. You were a spoiled kid who grew into a spoiled man, whose nasty ways have been coddled and overlooked by many for thirty plus years, so I can't really be mad at you for doing what you've been so accustomed to doing. My desire is that the man of God you say you are comes to life and lives for Christ wholeheartedly and stops pretending.

God bless you always, Big Fish.

I pray you submit...

16

I See You

WHERE DID IT ALL BEGIN? It began the day I opened my eyes. My destiny was already set in motion and the gifts God had given to me were irreversible. Ever since I was a young girl, I've seen things that others had no idea I saw. I am a seer, *not a physic, medium, person of intuition, or tarot card reader*, because that is not of God, *but of the devil.* A seer is one who God allows to see passed what the natural eye can see. This person is able to see beyond the surface, even to the spirit of a man or woman. Sounds a little scary right? Well, please know that you're not the only one it scared. The first time I started seeing the spirit of people, it bugged me out! As they stood before me, people who once were perfectly normal now appeared distorted. I thought I was losing my mind!

I remember my first run in with seeing spirits. I was at an industry party. There I was standing in the midst of all these well-known celebrities and a person walked up to give me a hug. Immediately their face became distorted as if they were some sort of monster. I almost jumped out of my pants! I played it off as much as I could asking myself, *What was that?* A few moments later, I went to speak to another person and saw the same thing! By this time I was scared to death, so I got out of there. I was petrified! I had no idea what was happening and that's when God gave me this understanding. He was allowing me to see the depths of who people really were and what was really around me.

Due to fear, I didn't want to see it anymore, so I asked God to take it away and he did. As I grew in God and became more mature, I realized this was something I needed to know. It was a vantage point for me to know exactly who and what was around me, so I asked God to forgive me for being afraid of the gift he gave and to restore it back to me. Thankfully, he did.

> I want to take a moment to teach this little nugget. God tells us specifically in his word, the Bible, not to seek out, or go after psychics, mediums, persons of intuition, or tarot card readers, because it is of the demonic realm. If you didn't know that psychics and the others that I've named are operating from the demonic realm, you now have an

understanding. Let this serve as a warning for you to stay away from such people.

There was a time in my life when I didn't know this truth and I reached out to a psychic to tell me my future. She was very general with the things she spoke of, but there were some things she shared that did come to pass. One thing about the devil is he poses as an angel of light, but that dude is the father of lies. *He is counterfeit.* You have to remember that a lie stems from the truth, but it's twisted. The devil has a way of making things appear to be true, which lures you into his plan. Once sucked in, his agenda is to control and devour you.

My Thought Process

I have no idea as to why I've always been considered the dumb, stupid, naïve, or gullible girl. Maybe it's because I never spoke up for myself or made people aware of the things I knew and saw within them. It's sad to say, but there are numerous people who think they've pulled the wool over my eyes but that wasn't or isn't the case. *I saw through your Maybelline*! I just chose not to say anything.

In some instances, I regret not opening my mouth. I cannot stomach the idea of someone thinking they've gotten one over on me. If only they knew what these eyes have truly seen, I'm sure they'd reconsider how they approach me. I'm not slow at comprehending. On the contrary, I catch on rather quickly and I attribute this to God's insight. I must say, there have been times, more than what I would like to admit, that I've made the choice to turn my face from the truth I saw in people. Maybe I chose to ignore them because I wanted them to fit into the mold of my life. Or maybe it was really because I didn't want people to be mad at me. I wanted everyone to like Pam. *Dang, that sounds about right.* But to those of you, who thought and still think that your girl is dumb, please don't get it twisted. I see you.

My eyes have seen and witnessed so much, yet I've remained quiet. For whatever reason I kept things to myself even when some of these same people began to talk and spread rumors about me as I got older. If only they knew, that I knew of their hidden secrets, they might not have been as vocal when it came to me having certain hang-ups. Maybe they would have second-guessed and refrained from some of the hurtful things they spoke about me in and out of public. Even though I had all the ammunition to take down an entire army, I zipped my lip. Silence was my portion.

It's funny how people think at times. Some have the arrogance to believe they can out charm the world. They put on this big front concerning the things they won't ever do, and how they can't believe how people could stoop so low and do some of the things that they do. *How quickly you've forgotten your past and the things you have partaken in.* I still have a fresh picture in my mind of everything you thought was under the radar. The things you believed no one would ever find out. Little did you know I saw you, and I saw you with my own eyes. I'm not here to put you on blast or to start calling out names because that's not my style but what I will say is, "*Stop!*" Stop throwing stones because you also live in a glass house, and a very fragile one at that. You should be very careful when it comes to pointing the finger. While you're pointing and shaking your one finger at others, you have three pointing back at you. Is your house really in order? Is there some dirt you've forgotten about that still resides on your jacket? As Martin Lawrence would say, "Silence!"

Getting a Clear View

I want to bring you into my world and disclose some of the things I've seen from a young girl to this present day. Some have been scary, some amusing, hurtful, rewarding, pleasurable, confusing, and some I've even used for my own plans. *I'm just being honest.* I dare not play the victim because in some of these situations I was trying to get something out of the ordeal as well. *You'll see.* I wasn't as innocent as I looked back then. I too had some things up my sleeve. A lot of people had me pegged wrong when they thought I was gullible and naïve. They had and still have no idea I was steps ahead of them. I could see the lust, the curiosity, the anger, the lies that they spoke, the fake smiles and so on and so forth. But I chose to let them believe something different, and that's what made me stupid, not naïve.

I recall playing house with friends as a little girl. There was a mother, a father, and kids, but one thing was missing, we didn't have a boy to play the daddy. Even though we didn't have a boy around it didn't stop our flow. Because we were all girls someone would just have to play the daddy role. Things got quite interesting a few times. I usually played the kid, but of course I wanted to be the grown-up. I saw the things that grown-ups did, so I would rather play that role. I wanted to play the grown-up because they told the kids what to do and we had to adhere. But there were also some things the grown-ups did that I wasn't supposed to see. The grown-ups kissed, played under the covers, and laid on top of one another. *Wait!* I just said there were no boys involved in the house playing. I saw girls kissing girls before I was ten years old. I would play sleep and watch what was going on. This made me want to be a grown-up whenever the game of house was played. I'm not going to get too deep into this, but what I will say is, some of these same girls ridiculed me when they found out I was dating girls for a season in my life. Did you forget when we played house? Have you forgotten how you were humping and kissing on girls? Maybe you forgot, or either you choose not to remember how you used to get down, but I didn't. I saw the kissing, the touching, and the laying on top of each other ya'll did. I'm not here to expose you, but I am exposing the truth about the things I saw. Hopefully by me doing so, you'll take a good look in the mirror and realize you're not everything you portray to be.

#CalmDown

As the years went by my mom finally allowed me to stay over a few of my friend's houses, but she was very selective as to where I could stay. If it wasn't family, I couldn't spend the night and honestly, she was indecisive with some of them. I had a great mom. She didn't play when it came to protecting her babies. She did all she could to make sure our environment was safe and conducive to children.

Now around this time I was hanging with girls who were considered grown women. They were eighteen and up and I was the young buck of the crew, but I was in the mix and happy about it. The reason why I was able to go and spend the night with them was because my mom trusted these girls. She felt like I wouldn't be hurt or influenced wrongly by them. This particular night seemed to be like any other night. We hung out, went to a friend's house, smoked a little weed, joked around until it was time for bed, and after that it was lights out. I don't remember if I was sleeping on the floor, couch, or a second bed in the room, but I do know I slept on something. *You know how you get so sleepy you don't remember falling asleep? I* guess that's what happened, or maybe it was because of the weed that I puffed on that put me out. All I know is I woke up in the middle of the night to this terrifying sight. Just so you know, I was only fifteen. I woke up and saw this woman, *a grown behind woman*, get up out the bed that my two friends were in. She was wearing nothing except panties. I quickly closed my eyes and played sleep.

Good thing she didn't walk close by where I was sleeping, because she would have heard my heart pounding and screaming, "I want to go home!" *What is going on?* Why are my friends in the bed with this woman? If you don't already know, I was ready to get out of there! It was too late to call home, but the next day, I was out!

Neither one of my friends knew that I saw this because I laid there, like a corpse, at shock of what I saw. This was crazy! What were they doing, and why did I have to see this? That image played in my head for such a long time. I couldn't get past wanting to know why my friends were in the bed with her.

At any rate, I'll stop there, but I will let you know

this. One of the friends that was in the bed with this woman used to judge so many things that I did. *Are you for real*? I never said anything concerning what I saw, I just let it go. I have no idea why I never brought it up especially when she would come at me running her mouth about what I did or didn't do. It's something how some people get amnesia when it comes to their secrets but are locked, loaded, and ready to shoot and judge everything you do. As far as I know, she is a woman who sleeps with men *only.* She made sure that this was something she said when trying to be funny and come for me. Well, I heard your bold statement, but I saw no naked man emerging from that bed on that night. It was surely a woman. I don't question your stance, nor am I saying you like women, but I do encourage you to be careful talking about other people's skeletons when you have a few bones yourself.

Throughout the course of my life, I have seen so much, but I have no clue as to why I saw it. I wasn't looking for it, but I did see it. *Most of the time I denied it.*

I've seen many heterosexual men *so they say,* gaze at another man when he walked into the room. As I stood in awe from disbelief, I never said a word. I watched as grown men's eyes danced and glared with lust at another man. I've witnessed the curiosity in the eyes of women who say they would never let a woman touch them. I've seen their thoughts of wanting to be involved, despite their outer display of disgust. *Remember when I said that there were some things I used for my own agenda, and that I wasn't innocent.* This is one of the areas I was referring to.

When I saw a woman who had curiosity, I played on it. I didn't play on it to be involved with them sexually. *I wasn't that person to sleep with everything and everyone, but I did have a big ego problem.* If I could just get their attention and then walk away, I was good. This was all due to my self-esteem issues, which we already discussed in the previous chapter.

I've also seen visions flash before me while awake. *Let me give you an example of what I'm speaking of.* I was sitting in my car one day in the summer with my windows down. As I sat there, I saw a vision of two guys walking toward my car. There was one guy walking in the street and the other was on the sidewalk. The guy on the sidewalk had a mean look on his face and the guy in the street came walking pass my window. The guy in the street pulled out a gun and shot me in the head, and the vision was over. Once I came out of it and was back in real time, I was very frightened *to say the least.* I started my car and pulled off. It was God warning me because I always sat in my car and read, slept, or relaxed. To my knowledge I didn't know people were watching and plotting against me, but God did.

This next situation is still a doozy for me. *It was heart wrenching and heart breaking. I lost who I thought was my brother and others, but loosing you hurt the most.* I sometimes still feel the pain from your absence but turning back is not an option. I'd rather hurt for a moment then ignore what I see any longer.

For a long time, you operated in deceit. And I kept quiet because I had hopes that what I was seeing in you was wrong, *but shame on me for not accepting your truths.* My mom used to say, "If it quacks like a duckwalks like a duck, then it's a duck." *No longer do I have to eat the whole cow to understand I'm eating beef.* Out of all people, I never thought it would have been you who'd betray me. I won't say that you didn't have me fooled for a while because you were good. You knew exactly how to pull me in with your charm and witty ways. By no means is that a compliment. You are deceiving and manipulative. *What an ugly combination.* I call you such names because I'm able to identify these spirits because I once was a carrier of the same ones. But the difference between you and I, is that. I wanted to change, and you enjoy operating in yours.

You have been deceiving yourself for so long, that you truly believe your ways are hidden, but they are bleeding out. Those that are close to you don't say it to your face. But most of your boys say that you are a crooked dude and that your ways are wrong. *I've gotten random calls from people wanting to get at you and my reply has been, "I'm praying and I'm sorry to hear that."* The pride and arrogance that you walk in makes dudes want to lay you out. Please wake up and smell yourself because you have an odor. You're leaking and making a mess of yourself everywhere. You speak one thing from the right side of your mouth and in the same breath, the left side speaks another.

Your double-lipped conversations have been exposed to me. All I could do is stand there and shake my head *when I heard it* because I know how you talk. So, when I was enlightened about a few conversations you had with others concerning me, I could hear your voice. I knew they weren't lying about the things they shared, but knew that if I approached you with questions, you would have lied, so I kept my mouth closed and just watched.

I had no idea you were a chameleon. You knew just when to change your colors so that you'd fit into every environment. Well my friend, you no longer fit into my life because I'm tired of being burned by someone who says that they love me. I saw the word *user* on you for a long time, but I didn't want to accept that that could really be your make up, *but it is.* Your love for me had grown throughout the years, but it has always been attached to a plan that was suitable for you. I know me taking a stance blows you away, because you can no longer get in.

I'm finally harkening to what I see.

Right now, you're not good for me, and who's to say that you'll ever be, but I do encourage you to let the act go. While writing my book, one of my cousins who were really close to my mom from out of nowhere shared my mom's views of you with me. His reason for contacting me was due to a post that I commented on, on social media. His words to me were, and I quote. "I am so happy you got this person out of your life. Your mom talked about him to me years ago. She told me how she couldn't wait for you to get this person out of your life because they meant you no good." She said, all they do is take from her. She pays everything for everybody, and I can't wait for her to get rid of them. Do you remember the day you asked me, "What would my mom say if she knew we wasn't close any more," I believe you finally got your answer and so did I.

I'd like to leave you with this thought. We all reap what we sow, so don't be surprised when you reap a harvest of what you've dealt to others. I'm not speaking a curse over you, I'm just saying what God says, and believe me it's true. I had to deal with my own reaping of doing others wrong at a point in my life. Just as sure as the sun rises, you'll taste the fruit of what you've planted in the ground. This doesn't just apply to you, but it is true for every human being. My only regret is that, had I told you in the beginning what I saw in you, maybe none of these things would have happened. It may have been a different outcome. Not sure of that, *because you are who you are*, but it was a thought…

My final words to those who know what you know. Never again close your eyes to it. What you see is being shown to you for a reason. Don't negotiate with yourself, and don't let people tell you that you're wrong when you know you're right. *You know what you saw!* So, believe it and then ask God what's next.

#Exposed

17

Be Free

AS I SIT AND THINK of the Emancipation Proclamation, I can't even imagine how the slaves felt to finally hear that they were free. Free from the bondage of others, and free from being forced to comply with things that diminished their worth. The thirst that they had for freedom was now within their grasp. After all the deaths, whips, chains, escapes, captures, and tears the slaves endured, in January 1863, 3.1 million slaves out of 4 million were freed. *What was that day like*? How did it feel to walk away and know that what once held you down, no longer had a right to touch you? *Was it just a day of total jubilee, or was there some fear of the unknown in the atmosphere?* Just think about how much joy they felt knowing they were free, and yet with the same weight that they had from joy. *I believe,* there also lingered the fear of what was to come. There were many slaves that had freedom before they were captured and sold into slavery, so living free was somewhat already experienced by some. However, I believe most were born into slavery rather than those who were captured. With this being the case, just picture slavery being all that one knows and in one day, *bam*! You're able to go free. That would be scary for any person.

Sometimes change has the power to make a person grow cold *due to fear*. You know in your heart that you want to be free, and you've even seen yourself being free, but taking the steps to freedom sometimes is the hardest part. It's hard because you leave behind everything your life was based upon. The foundation that you once knew has to be demolished and rebuilt from the ground up and that is not easy. *The rebuilding process takes time.*

Today, we live in a society that says, "I need it right now," or else we're not interested. This mentality has caused us to become slaves unknowingly. We may say that we are not slaves but walk with me to see if that's the case. I initially disagreed, but when I looked a little closer, bondage was my middle name. And anything that has a person bound, makes them a slave to it.

I know a good bit of you probably want to close this book right now because you don't agree with me on this one, but I guarantee if you do some self-evaluation you'll see, what I saw within myself, as well. There are so many of us who are afraid to be the real us. We look at others and desire what they have or who they are. Instead of being authentic, we'd rather try to duplicate what is being done.

Have you ever stopped to consider the person who you think has it all together? We slightly envy them from afar because in our eyes, they appear to be the marquee of excellence. Our thoughts are consumed with believing they have the best of everything; the job, the car, the house, the kids and etc. We study them not to learn, but to become. Due to their outward appearances we conclude they have it all and that life is awesome, but is that really the case? Underneath their many layers could lie a soul ready to throw in the towel on life. We have no idea that they could be seconds away from a mental breakdown. We, could very well be one of the ones who they've been waiting on. Someone to help lead them out of captivity, but because we are bound by appearances, we don't even realize that we've been called to lead, and not conform. We may no longer have chains on our wrist, but our minds are chained by what we see. And that my friend, is enslavement.

There is nothing wrong with wanting more, but the motive behind it all is key. We want more because we're fixated on what the next person has, and we're doing all that we can to look, sound, and be just like them. All we're doing is following behind a master, and if a person has a master, then you are a slave! *Ouch! This hit me hard as well.* I had to eat this truth and it wasn't the most appetizing, but it yielded something in me that no one could take away. But before growth could come, I first had to admit that I was a slave.

So many of us are weighed down by our past. And it is hindering and holding us from our growth and future. Our eyes have grown dim and our hope has become second to none. Being a carbon copy of someone has become the way of life for so many people. We have given up on the mere thought of living a life of fulfillment and wholeness because we actually have to stand up and fight for it. We would rather be a duplicate than be ourselves because being ourselves seems to have no value. The devil is a liar! You have so much to offer. If only you could see yourself free from the images of this world and its perceptions, you could live a life that has the potential to soar. You were created to be peculiar and not common, so get your focus off of others and start embracing you. Someone is waiting on what you have. It's time for you to stop living beneath your worth and settling.

Please understand that the steps to freedom are not always easy but they yield everlasting results. I won't lie to you and say that it doesn't come with a price tag because it does. Stepping out may possibly cost you everything, but it's so worth it. When I began to walk my path to freedom. I wanted to turn back so many times because I saw things in me I didn't know existed, but I had to keep walking. I knew if I could get free from comparison and wanting what others had, every misconception I had of myself would have to loose me and let me go. This was not an easy process at all. But as I fought, with tear's running down my face, I was determined to become emancipated by any means necessary, even if this meant exposing me.

Opening up the chambers of your heart will never be easy, but your pain can help someone else gain freedom. Knowing that you're not alone in a situation has the power to strengthen others to tell their story and heal wounded souls. I'm not saying that we find joy in another person's pain *because that's foolish.* But what I am saying is, your truth has the power to help give someone else the strength to move past his or her devastation and become a victor instead of a victim.

When we begin to understand that the things we've been through don't have to rule our lives. I believe that's when freedom begins to have its perfect work within us. *You have the right to be free!* You were not created to be bound! Life can and will begin again if you so choose. It's time for NEW!

New life.

New love.

New joy.

New peace.

New outlook.

New outcome.

New ________ _________ You fill in the blanks!

This is your moment! You have to start with you!

Say It with Me

I am new! I am no longer a slave! I am free!

This journey has caused old wounds to be reopened and old feelings I thought were dead, to emerge. But that's not where my story ends. I have become victorious over things that I was bound by for years. My strength to stand has birthed forth victory. I no longer have to hide or be silent about my past, because I am finally free. No longer do people have to play the guessing game when it comes to me. Every question that they've ever had concerning my life now has an answer. I refuse to hide any longer. What's interesting is that I wasn't really hiding from people, I was hiding from myself. I had become so consumed with other people's opinions of me that I became a slave to unknown masters. People were controlling me, and they didn't even know it, *but no more!* Today is a new day. I am willing to change, and I am ready for change. *In my Apostle DD voice.* My wings have expanded, and this butterfly has broken out from the fight within that dark cocoon and I smell roses. It's time for me to fly to the heights I've been called too, so that I can show others how to do the same.

You no longer have to walk alone. God heard your cry.

18

The Most Beautiful Girl in the World

WHAT CAN I SAY to describe the most breathtaking woman I've ever seen? The love we shared will always remain written within my being. I can't completely recall the day we met, but there is one thing I know for sure. *I'll never forget you.* Even though you're physically gone your presence will forever engulf my heart. *You were perfect.* Not in the sense of you doing everything correctly, but your perfection was in your imperfections. They set you apart and gave you such a distinction. How about those pigeon-toed, bowed legs of yours? When you walked, those legs *of yours* made it seem as if you were going to trip yourself. And what about your front tooth that slightly overlapped the other one, *just a tad bit.* These are just two small infractions that made you uniquely perfect. No one would ever know because you downplayed your beauty.

If only you could have seen what I saw when I looked at you. Your beauty was radiant like the sun. Your frame was thick but petite. Your skin was dark, smooth, butter soft, and without a blemish. Your chinky and bright puppy dog eyes, *which had little slants in the corner*, were so inviting. And that pearly white million-dollar smile was all people talked about. Even your scent was distinct and definably noticeable. *So much so*, that when you walked into a room not only was your presence felt, but your sweet aroma was in the air.

You were also an eye catcher. *Gorgeous*! Everybody knew who Miss Judy was and that wasn't because you wanted to be seen. All who knew you knew you were shy and always in the cut. The reason why you stood out so much was because of the selflessness you displayed toward others. Everybody loved you. *You were a household name in our community.*

I even remember how the guys, both young and old talked about how nice looking and well put together Miss Judy was. There were times when I overheard conversations being had about you that made me have to interrupt to say, "Yes, my mama is beautiful," as I smiled. You were what they called a "bad mamma jamma," and they were not exaggerating. Miss Judy was a hottie that could have had her pick of the litter, but the awesome thing about it was, you never played into any of it. You remained humble and did what you did best, and that was taking care of your babies and being our mama.

To tell you the truth, I never intended on implementing you in the pages of this book because I always thought you would be here giving me pointers as I wrote it. But since things have changed, I knew I had to share the love I've had the opportunity of knowing, from such a beautiful damsel. You truly were my rose out of concrete.

I finally understand what you meant when you used to say, "Don't take me for granted." I am so glad that as I grew up, I learned how to appreciate you, because in my younger years I couldn't understand why you were so overprotective. I felt like I couldn't do anything, and I remember saying to myself that I wished someone else was my mom. Of course, you didn't hear me say that because if you had, I would have been eating your fist. You would have made it a point that my butt would never allow my mouth to speak those words again. I'm so glad you didn't hear me. *That's one less whoopin on my record.*

As I began to understand that love not only gives but protects and has many dimensions, *which you displayed,* I began to think of you differently. The more I matured, the more I realized that I had someone great in my midst. Receiving this revelation made me want to give you everything. You sacrificed so much so we could have, that now it was my turn to do it for you.

How about the times we sat down to eat, and you made sure our plates were full as you nibbled on the little leftovers in the pot? Because of how I saw you deny yourself, I felt like it was my duty to always be there for you because that's what you did for me. *I wasn't going to do anything less.* My father ran away from his responsibility to love and care for me, and you could have done the same, but you opted to stay. You made a conscience decision to love me every day no matter how hard it got, and that made me love you like you were my own flesh.

Just thinking of you causes my cheekbones to rise. The smile that illuminates my face at the mention of your name professes to everyone who sees it that you were, and forever will be my favorite girl. There is not another person breathing on the face of this earth that could ever compare to the love I felt and knew from you. We were like two peas in a pod, inseparable. Well at least I didn't want to be separated from you. *I clung to your every move.* I told you early on, at a young age, that you weren't getting rid of me. I guess you didn't take me seriously, but as the years went by, I stuck to my word. I was like a fly on doo-doo when it pertained to you. I could smell you from miles away and I made it my business to be where you were. When you turned to the right, I was there. When you turned to the left, there I stood. And when you wanted your quiet time, I tried my best not to intervene. Everything you were, I wanted to become. You were my superhero. The only thing missing was the red cape, which I believe you wore under your clothes because I don't know how you made ends meet back then, but somehow you did. You were dynamic! All I ever saw you be was a mother who took great care of her babies and because of that I vowed to give you the world. Whatever it would take to make you happy I was willing to go the distance. You deserved that and more.

Not only were you a mother to us, you even mothered other people's kids and treated them just like they were your own. Sometimes I felt like telling them to go and get their own mommy because you were mine, but I now know you were created to be who you were, *a help to those in need.* You gave your all to everyone, *especially us,* and never went looking for anything in return. I believe that's what prompted me to say as a little girl, "I'm going to break my back trying to make sure my mama is happy, and she'll never have to want for anything!" All I knew was that I had the best, and my job was to replicate what was given to me. I wasn't saying this from a place of obligation nor compulsion, but from a place of love. Love moves a person into action and that's exactly what you did for me. I had to show up for the one that showed up for me. Everything that you were I wanted to become.

I remember growing up and hearing people say that I looked like my father and I would get so mad! I wanted them to say that I looked like you. Why would I want to look like someone I only saw whenever I would visit our family in North Carolina for the summer? *He didn't love me. At least that's what I believed.* But I knew you loved me. I knew I could count on you. I knew that you would always be there, and I also knew you would never let me down. With that being said, I wanted to look like the one I knew. Honestly speaking, I do look like my dad, but as I've gotten older, I thank God for allowing me the privilege of finally resembling you. *Yes God!* I say privileged because I count it an honor to resemble you my queen. You were a special lady mom and to be able to look into the mirror and see a part of you in me, leaves me in awe.

As I sit and reminisce about who you were to me, my heart longs for you. The thoughts of you not being here formulate tears in my eyes. You weren't supposed to die! This was not a part of my plan! Super heroes don't perish! They may get tired and they may even get wounded, but death was never part of their DNA.

Sometimes I want to question God, but I know he knows best. It's just moments like this that sometimes make me want to question everything. Your death was a reality check for me. It made me understand that you were just as human as I am, and it also showed me. I must live life to its fullest potential because tomorrow is not promised. Upon you transitioning there was one thing God showed me that will remain with me always. I now know that whatever life throws I'll be able to face it head on, because for me to still be alive after losing my best friend shows me how God has made me army strong. *Dang Mommy!* I am so emotional right now. I miss you terribly! If only I could talk to you face-to-face one more time, I would spend the whole day telling you how much you mean to me. I would hug, kiss, and hold your hand for hours and make sure I told you everything in my heart. I would monopolize every second of our time together. Just to see that beautiful smile of yours, *that lit up my world,* would soothe my whole being. *Mommy! I miss you!*

No one can ever imagine how much I think about you. There are not many days that go by that I haven't desired for you to be here. Sometimes I feel lost because you were such a major part of me, but I thank God for you leaving me with something that has comforted my bleeding soul. You told me you weren't afraid to die and that you were going to see Jesus. You told me you would miss me, Beans and Tizzle but if it was time for you to go, you were ready. This is why in the midst of me yearning for you, I have peace. *I know where you are.* You are in the presence of the Lord and that's the best place, no matter how selfish I want to be and have you here with me.

The relationship/friendship we had was beautiful. I had the best of both worlds, but I knew not to ever cross the lines of dishonoring you as my mother. You taught me that friendships sometimes come to an end, but being my mother was perpetual. What that showed me was that, you and I could laugh and have fun all day, but if I ever got out of line, our friendship was over. I would quickly find myself in the hands of an angry mom who was about to teach my butt a lesson, *literally.* I knew better than to ever disrespect you. With the exception of when I was sixteen and thought I could talk back to you. *That's a day I'll never forget.* You beat me until you got tired. I remember Pop coming to the room door telling you it was enough, but you looked up at him with this look and he just walked away as you continued. All I will say is that after the whoopin you put on me, I never had to endure another one in my life. I would have rather bit my tongue off than to ever have gotten out of line with you again. You put a hurting on me that day and it knocked some sense into my hardhead.

You did not play when it came to us honoring you, you weren't going to have it any other way. You weren't striving to be my friend, but a mother who made sure I knew and respected every word you said. If I didn't, I would be sure to suffer the consequences. If for one moment I thought otherwise, those switches, belts, and hands coming across my butt brought me back to reality rather quickly. After things settled down you would explain to me why you whooped me, and you never failed to tell me that you loved me. In that moment, in my head, I would be like, "Yeah right! I hope you fall down the stairs!" But in my heart, I knew you loved me. *I was just mad that you beat me.*

Our relationship was strong and tight like a gnat's booty. Nothing could break us apart, not even death. I'm still Mommy's little girl and I'm still going hard for you. I want to make you happy and I want you to know that all your blood, sweat, and tears were not in vain. You were, and still are, the yin to my yang. I wanted to love and protect you the same way you did for me. I knew I could never match it, but I sure was trying too.

There were so many nights when I would come into your room just to make sure you were breathing. I would stand there and stare to see if your stomach was going up and down. Once I saw it, I would leave out of your room knowing that everything was okay. I had to make sure you were good. This was just me and God's little secret. Maybe I was made to watch out for you just as much as you were made to watch out for me. I don't know what prompted me to do this for so many years, but I never got tired of checking on you. Thinking back, I believe a good bit of it was fear of losing you and the other part was because I was being your protector. *I know that made God laugh*, because he was your protector, not me. There were some nights when I was trying to sleep in your bed, but when you woke up and caught me, you'd make me leave. *I would be infuriated!* I must admit there were some nights when you allowed me to stay, and I sure made the best of it. *You would have thought I was literally apart of your hip, that's how far up under you I would sleep.* God knows I loved/love you so much. Just thinking of you puts me at a loss for words, because nothing can truly describe the best mother in the world. You were a 24/7, 365 days of the year mom. When it came to parenting you gave all that you had and you also gave what you didn't. There was never a moment where I felt like you weren't there. You were always present, always in the now. When it came to your babies everything stopped. You even put away your happiness to make sure we could have a good life. You denied yourself so that we could have. Who does that? I know who does something like that—you.

Not only were you my champion/hero, you were my biggest cheerleader. When it came down to achieving my goals, you made me feel like I could do anything I put my mind to. You always helped me to see the bigger picture, and you also eased my mind to know that everything was going to be alright. Even when you knew we were facing tough times, you held fast to that beautiful smile of yours and assured us that all was well. *You never bailed out on me.* You stayed with me in the thick of things when everything looked impossible. When I told you that college wasn't for me and that I wanted to be a singer, your words to me were, "Okay, you can do it, boo." You believed in me from day one. I never felt that I had to abandon my dreams to become what you thought I should be, but instead you pushed me to go forward even more.

Most people don't have a clue that I get my singing and dancing from you. It was you who taught me how to sing on my first microphone, *i.e., a broomstick,* as we cleaned the house on Saturday mornings. The whole family cleaned with Smokey Robinson, Stephanie Mills, Marvin Gaye, and of course Michael Jackson blaring in the background. You showed me how to sing lead and how to sing the backgrounds. I can still see you singing and dancing right now. What a beautiful vision! No one but your babies had the privilege of seeing you do your thing on the mic, because of you being so shy. If only people could have been a fly on the wall, they would have seen one of the best! You not only groomed me for the real world, but God also used you to groom my singing career at a young age. You were involved in every area of my life. It's something how you don't see or acknowledge those things when you're younger, but as you grow, the picture becomes a whole lot clearer. I truly get it from my mama.

What an amazing woman you were? Not only did you see me through the good times, but you were even closer through the bad. I think back on all the times you stood by me when my life was in shambles. Everything and everyone had disappeared except my day one. There was not a rose in sight and everything around me was thorny, but you showed me how to stand strong, and how to hold onto hope. You encouraged me when all seemed lost. When I hit rock bottom you loved me more and helped to nurse me back to life. You showed me whether I'm at the top of the charts or working at a fast food restaurant, I was still your baby. You reminded me that it wasn't about what I had that defined me, but the definition of who I was *and am*, is from God and God only. If only people knew the storms you suffered through with me, *they would quickly agree with who I say you are.* I bless God for strengthening you to stand by my side the way you did.

I remember looking at you one day and seeing the heaviness lifted from your countenance. All I could do was give God praise. Your prayers had been answered and your peace came rushing back to you because your baby had finally given her life to Christ. I could look into your eyes and see that you knew Jesus was taking great care of me. To see you not have to worry about me any longer was so beautiful. I remember when you shared with me that you were afraid for me because of me. *Wow*! Your fear had nothing to do with other people hurting me but all to do with what I had the potential of doing to myself. I had become my biggest enemy. I remember when God allowed you to finally have peace in knowing that he had me, because you finally stopped staying up to see if I made it home. You no longer had to take my car keys because of me being drunk. You began to trust me again. Not just trusting me but trusting God with me. I bless God for giving that to you. A mother's prayer helped to save her baby girl's life.

There is not another mom in this lifetime that I would have ever picked over you. We may not have been rich with finances, but we were surely rich in love. A blind man could see the love you showered down on your kids. You devoted your life to us.

Whatever you had to do, you did. You made it happen without my dad being around, and you never complained or spoke badly about him. You just did what needed to be done and allowed us to find out things on our own as we got older. The love you gave was, and still is, in full effect. You were infectious! You and God are the reason why I have this big heart. Your love cannot be hidden or denied. It was too strong for it not to be remembered or still felt.

I remember the day of your home going service. The church and streets were packed. You gave your own eulogy. Your life spoke volumes. I am forever in debt to you, Mommy. I owe it to you, to pay it forward. The legacy you left behind is a legacy that extends the love of God, and I must do the same. The Lord's name won't be in vain and neither will yours. I have my moments when my heart breaks because of me not being able to touch you physically, but there are times when I feel you near. When that happens, I immediately stop and say "Thank you Lord Jesus," because he knows what we need and just when to send it. You will forever be a major part of me, and I'm going to do everything I can to keep my promises to you. The torch has been passed down to me and I can't allow it to be blown out, *not on my watch.* I have to give what was freely given to me and that is love. If I live what you taught me, I'll be sure to keep your legacy going and it'll continue throughout our bloodline from generation to generation to generation, until God raptures the earth.

You were the epitome of the word "mother," and I thank you for never letting go, *of me. B*ecause had you let go, I may not have made it. I love you, Mom! I will always be your honeybun.

Until we meet again, my beautiful cupcake!

Outro

Even with all that I've been through, I'm still here. I have a purpose and so do you. God can heal you everywhere there is pain. All you have to do is come. He is a healer/deliverer. Jesus Christ the Son of God is the answer to your every need.

He loves you.

About the Author

Pamela Long was raised in Edison, New Jersey, by a single mother, where she is known for being "Judy's baby." She graduated from JPS high school and went on to superstardom as one of the three ladies that made up the R&B group Total.

Pamela has hit stages throughout the world and sung on some of the biggest hit records of our time. Her vocals are featured on "Hypnotized" with The Notorious B.I.G and on countless other records with elite artists.

Pamela Long is known for her ability to pull an audience into her world from the passion she puts out on stage. She was born to perform, and she won't be stopping anytime soon. Recognized by millions as the girl with the distinct voice, she is now using that same sound the world fell in love with to tell her story—with the hopes of untying others from their past.

.

Connect with Pamela

INSTAGRAM: instagram.com/PamelaLong4ever

FACEBOOK: facebook.com/officialpamelalong

TWITTER: twitter.com/pamelalong1

Acknowledgments

I want to thank my mom, Judith Long, for everything she's taught and given to me throughout my life, which was her all! I bless God for the life you decided to allow me to experience by not aborting me.

I know that one day we will meet again but until then, I'm going to do everything I can to make you proud.

I still love you with everything God has given me the power to love you with. That won't ever change. You are and will forever be my earthly everything! You are my hero, my sweetheart, and my cupcake. I love you, Mommy.

Before you left this life to journey on to eternity, you told me not to let anything get in my way (as you shed tears), not even what you were going through; and my words to you were, "I won't." As soon as I spoke those words, you quickly stopped crying.

So I say to you, my beautiful mommy (as Apostle DD would say), it's game time!

I will make you happy by the grace of God. You are and forever will be my favorite girl.

PS I still remember the promise you made me, and I am holding fast to it with everything I got. Because of you not liking to travel, you told me that when I begin to win the awards for my music (that I am destined for), you would be sitting in the front row cheering me on.

One thing I know about my mama is that you've always kept your word to your babies, so I'll be looking for you on that front row, and without a shadow of a doubt, I know you'll be there!

My queen of hearts for eternity. Your baby loves you, Mommy! Judy plus Pam equals God's Love.

God

To my Father, who has always had me in His arms. No matter what state or condition in life I found myself in, you have ALWAYS been there for me. I have no idea as to why you held on to me, but I'm so thankful that you never let me go. I feel like I have truly been one of the most hardheaded kids that you have, yet your love for me is consistent. Even when I had my moments of thinking that you were done with me, you always had a way of letting me know you still loved me.

True parents never give up on their kids even when it appears that things will never change. I was what many called a hellish teenager/young adult, but you saw the best in me.

You knew that if I opened up my heart and experienced real love that my life would never be the same. And because a good father will go to whatever extent needed to reach his child, I finally met *love* and my life has never been the same since that day.

You loved me so much that you gave your only Son to die for me on a cross so that I might live. Not only did you give me your best, you gave me your everything!

Thank you for never letting me go! I LOVE YOU, PAPA!

To Judy's Babies

I want to thank you for always standing by my side when everyone who claimed to love me left. No matter who/what entered or left my life, every time I looked up y'all have always been there and I am forever thankful to God for all of you. We may *at times* have our differences and our little squabbles, but the imprint of family is engraved in our hearts forever. We are and forever will be Judy's babies! God knew just what he was doing when he put all of us together.

To my big brother James (Beanie), aka my dude and the only father figure I knew. You have no idea what you mean to me. I love you from my heart. May you continue to push forward and be the example of greatness you're destined to be.

To Tabitha (Tizzle), the sister who always had my front, back, and sides. You were always the one who came to my rescue and laid jokas out with that left hook. I love you, Tgirl. You can do anything you put your mind to. Get up and go forward. You have so much waiting on you. Let's get it.

And to my beautiful nieces and handsome nephews, what would I do without you? I know you're older, but you're forever my babies. Words will never express what you mean to me.

Destiny (Wes), Chynah (Whiney), Xavier (Son), Jada (Mae) and Mehki (Khi): I know y'all are probably like, "Why she put our nicknames in this book?" Don't be mad. I love y'all so much. Please know that God has a plan for your lives. He has things in store for you that you can't even imagine. Tap in and let God blow your mind. Be the one amongst your peers they wanna imitate as you imitate Jesus Christ. Y'all were born to lead! Let's get it, my babies....

Tasha, Quilly, and Talahni

To my sister Tasha, whom I've known since I was eleven years old. Thank you for the unconditional love and sisterhood that will always remain. You've always pushed me to go after my dreams without fail. Thank you for being there through it all. I love you and Tyrone.

To my godchildren Quilly and Talahni. I love you both dearly. There is nothing that you can't do. Go for it! As long as you keep Jesus with you, all things are possible.

#familyforever

Apostle DD

To my pastor/sister/friend! I want to thank you for being you. By you being yourself sparked a flame in me to raise the bar in my life to truly become what God has called me to be.

You have no idea how much you've taught me how to believe in myself and to stand for the truth even if I'm standing alone, and for that I am forever grateful. You have seen the best and the worst of me. At times I'm pretty sure you could have walked away, but instead you stood flatfooted (as my friend) and told me the truth about myself. This caused me to have to look in the mirror and make the decision to change or stay the same. I chose the latter.

Thank you for frustrating, upsetting, and making me angry, but most of all helping me to understand that the sun didn't rise and set on Pam. *In other words, it was not about me.* You also explained to me that I could no longer be a people pleaser but a God pleaser. Real friends help one another give birth to what they've been called by God to do, and the baby is finally here! So again, I say thank you for pushing, dragging and kicking me into my destiny.

I love you, Apostle.